UNEXPECTED

Unexpected

Parenting, Prenatal Testing, and Down Syndrome

Alison Piepmeier

with George Estreich and Rachel Adams

NEW YORK UNIVERSITY PRESS

New York

NEW YORK UNIVERSITY PRESS
New York
www.nyupress.org

© 2021 by New York University
All rights reserved

References to internet websites (URLs) were accurate at the time of writing. Neither the author nor New York University Press is responsible for URLs that may have expired or changed since the manuscript was prepared.

Library of Congress Cataloging-in-Publication Data
Names: Piepmeier, Alison, author. | Estreich, George, editor. | Adams, Rachel, 1968–   editor.
Title: Unexpected : parenting, prenatal testing, and Down syndrome /
Alison Piepmeier, with George Estreich and Rachel Adams.
Description: New York : New York University Press, [2021] |
Includes bibliographical references and index.
Identifiers: LCCN 2020016531 (print) | LCCN 2020016532 (ebook) | ISBN 9781479816637
(cloth) | ISBN 9781479879953 (paperback) | ISBN 9781479865468 (ebook) | ISBN
9781479827183 (ebook)
Subjects: LCSH: Mothers of children with Down syndrome. | Motherhood. |
Prenatal diagnosis. | Children with Down syndrome. | Family planning—
Decision making. | Sociology of disability.
Classification: LCC RJ506.D68 P53 2021 (print) | LCC RJ506.D68 (ebook) |
DDC 618.92/858842—dc23
LC record available at https://lccn.loc.gov/2020016531
LC ebook record available at https://lccn.loc.gov/2020016532

New York University Press books are printed on acid-free paper, and their binding materials are chosen for strength and durability. We strive to use environmentally responsible suppliers and materials to the greatest extent possible in publishing our books.

Manufactured in the United States of America

10 9 8 7 6 5 4 3 2 1

Also available as an ebook

Frontispiece: Alison Piepmeier, October 2013. Source: Staff, The College of Charleston.

for Maybelle

CONTENTS

Preface

Alison Piepmeier was a scholar of literature, feminism, and disability studies; a prolific columnist and blogger; an activist; a beloved professor and mentor; and a parent. For Alison, these roles and categories were interconnected, so it is unsurprising that in her last and most ambitious work, she tried to draw these strands together: to write a book that included personal witness and analytical rigor, that fused an activist's fire, a poet's eye, and a scholar's care. The manuscript was left incomplete when Alison died of brain cancer, at the age of forty-three, in August 2016.

Before she died, Alison and George communicated by email, then by Skype, about the possibility of his completing the project. Realizing the dimensions of the project and the expertise required, George told Alison that he wanted to bring on their mutual friend Rachel as a coeditor. Rachel, Alison, and George had known each other for years. Like Alison, Rachel and George each have a child with Down syndrome; like Alison, they have written publicly about the experience of parenting, linking it to questions of disability. Rachel's training in disability studies, feminism, and literature was a perfect complement to the expertise George could contribute to this project. Alison gave her enthusiastic approval to the idea, and Rachel accepted, with equal enthusiasm.

This book is our attempt to complete the manuscript in accordance with Alison's wishes. It's mainly composed of Alison's writing—an assembly that highlights the best of her work, in line with the structure she had set out. Each of us has also contributed a chapter about an aspect of Alison's work, offering context and appreciation for her achievement.

* * *

In a blog post published shortly after Alison died, her husband Brian McGee wrote, "To share a life with Alison Piepmeier was to be constantly aware of her uneasy relationship with time." He spoke of "Alison's unaffected brilliance" and added that "wit and erudition weren't sufficient to make her the enthusiastic presence, the cheerful dynamo so many of us came to adore. Often, it was Alison's anxious awareness of the passage of time that provided the abundance of energy she channeled so effectively to teach, to serve her community, to mentor students—and always, always, to write. It was Alison's anxious awareness of time that frequently had her finishing tasks and moving on to the next challenge hours or days before deadlines."[1]

Alison was diagnosed with a brain tumor in early 2010. She died in August 2016. As Brian wrote, her illness "changed her relationship with time"—not only in symptoms, side effects, and radical shifts in her daily routines, but also in facing the shock of medical prediction. "She had to live with the ability of medical professionals to predict, however imperfectly, the most likely dates of her demise. . . . Focus was never Alison's problem, but nothing was quite so focusing as her physician's affidavit stating that she had 6–12 months to live."

Brian put his finger on the distinctive temporalities of illness and disability that writers like Alison Kafer, Ellen Samuels, and Robert McRuer call "crip time."[2] Borrowing from queer theory, these scholars observe that illness and disability can make time slow down or speed up, move backward or sideways, or repeat itself, confounding traditional notions of progress, development, and uniformity. Alison worked with the queer-crip understanding that she might not have the gradual, elongated unfolding of a conventional life span. She lived with the patient's sense that time is not her own, given how much of it is spent waiting in the shadow cast by the uncertain pronouncements of medical professionals. She also lived with an awareness of how unpredictable a body can become, as the threat of exhaustion and debility challenges the attempt to plan a future program of research and writing. These unusual temporalities can make queer-crip writing feel open-ended, unpolished, and raw. They also invite us to think about the devices used by those who are healthy and able-bodied to mask the fact that all futures are uncertain.

Reading Alison's drafts of the chapters that became this book, we kept tripping over markers of the unfinished. Both the wit and the hurry, the urgency of prognosis and the linguistic skill she brought to it—a skill under siege by the very illness she sought to narrate—are evident in the placeholders embedded in her drafts:

No epigraph yet.
  Brilliant person
  But. . . . [transition]
  Another person said xxx.
  BOOK: Nameless.

That urgency—"always, always to write"—marks her notes to herself, her assessments of what the book was, and was becoming. Her notes mark time and are marked by the consciousness of time: "Synthesis as of 3:00 on May 12," she wrote to herself once. She was keenly aware of the book as an evolving thing, and in her notes, we see a conversation with herself, an urgent meditation on the book's direction.

Alison's original book proposal, shared with us by her editor Ilene Kalish, focused on reproductive decision-making, in Alison's words, "a feminist disability studies examination of decisions parents and potential parents have to make." At that time, the book's proposed title was *A Choice with No Story: What Prenatal Testing and Down Syndrome Reveal about Our Reproductive Decision-Making.* That focus on reproductive decision-making grew out of Alison's experiences of pregnancy, birth, and motherhood with Maybelle, who has Down syndrome. It also grew from her extensive interviews of mothers who, facing a diagnosis of

Down syndrome in utero, chose either to continue pregnancies or to terminate. As Alison's original title implies, the mothers attempting to make sense of this situation did so in the absence of narrative—or, more precisely, in the presence of conflicting narratives about the meaning and value of a child with Down syndrome.

In an enthusiastic review of the book proposal for New York University Press, Rachel called Alison's work "an important and timely project." She described it as a study of prenatal testing that would collect "the rarely-heard stories of parents and prospective parents who have confronted decisions about a fetus diagnosed with Down syndrome. [Alison] questions the rhetoric of 'choice' that surrounds prenatal testing, showing how decisions are shaped and limited by familial and cultural attitudes, as well as available resources. Although prenatal testing is designed to detect a range of genetic conditions, the book zeroes in on Down syndrome because it so often becomes the exclusive focus of the rhetoric and popular understanding of genetic tests."

In the fall of 2015, editors and other reviewers shared Rachel's enthusiasm, and soon the project was under contract. Though Alison questioned how much of the manuscript would be personal, or how the personal and the academic modes would fit together, she was clearly moving toward memoir, focusing on her own experience of motherhood and illness:

> Chapter 5—sitting/eating together. We're together @ a moment of sadness. How much should this be about me? How much of any of this is me? What emphasis? I think the emphasis always has to come back to MB [Maybelle], and my head.
>
> But I do think our scholarship is crucial. Who do I see? How does their work connect to what I'm exploring?

"MB, and my head": these words could be taken as shorthand for two aspects of Alison's life. She was a parent and a patient, and as such, she

Maybelle and Alison Piepmeier. Source: Trey Piepmeier

realized that her daily life was permeated by unanswerable questions. What is the line between illness and disability? How did Alison's challenges with language, brought on by a brain tumor, differ from Maybelle's, associated with Down syndrome?

Alison had always explored other kinds of writing. She wrote poetry in college, and as George argues in his chapter, her blog contains some of her best writing. Read in sequence, the blog entries can be understood as a single essay. (Indeed, the blog can be seen as a proving ground for this book, a place to mix the minutiae of everyday life with feminist analysis.) But for Alison, this was a new kind of book. It both differs from, and grows out of, her work on nineteenth-century women's writing (*Out in Public: Configurations of Women's Bodies in Nineteenth-Century America*); on zines (*Girl Zines: Making Media, Doing Feminism*); or, with co-editor Rory Dicker, on third-wave feminism (*Catching a Wave: Reclaiming Feminism for the 21st Century*). It shares with previous work her interest in women, the body, popular culture, and activism.

From the beginning, her insights about gender were inflected by an understanding of the intersections of race and class. As a scholar trained in literary studies, Alison was keenly aware that representations matter. Not only do they reflect prevailing social beliefs, but they also have the power to unsettle, and even transform, dominant attitudes. She was interested in women as social and historical agents, as makers and doers actively engaged in shaping the realities under which they lived. Alison also knew that feminist knowledge is situated knowledge. Even at her most scholarly, she was always present in her writing—her vivid sense of voice and her passions, commitments, and beliefs evident on the page. Her new book was meant to connect her scholarly and theoretical preoccupations with her personal experience and to reach beyond a purely academic audience.

As Alison's conception of the book evolved, the idea of story remained, a common thread among her varied approaches. She was fascinated by the power of narrative to help and to harm. A parent's experiences can yield stories that dehumanize their subjects, particularly in the case of intellectual disability, but a different story about the same experiences can recognize dignity and personhood, replacing reduction with complexity. As Alison showed in her study of parent memoirs, these opposing impulses often coincide. While Alison never had the chance to fully theorize her interest in narrative, her approach was in keeping with scholarship in disability studies and medical humanities that recognizes the power of personal stories to serve as a kind of embodied theory. As Elaine Scarry wrote in her influential study *The Body in Pain*, although pain is a source of unmaking that robs the subject of language, the world is remade through artistic creation.[3]

Alison understood the inevitability of story, the way it functions to organize experience and beliefs.[4] She recognized how those who have experienced pain or oppression use narrative to make and to remake an imperfect social world. Her work intersected with the project of narrative medicine in acknowledging the reparative power of telling stories and learning how to listen and interpret the stories of others.[5]

A particular concern in this book is how women use stories to organize their experiences of pregnancy and motherhood. Alison sees how the memoir can challenge well-known narratives about illness and disability, redefining what it means to live with physical and cognitive differences. In this book, Alison analyzes stories about disability, pregnancy, and motherhood but also tells stories of her own. For Alison, narrative at its best is the agent of complexity; in her evolving manuscript, she takes a complex approach, both as storyteller and as critic. Her primary commitment in this book is to understand the capacity of stories to work imaginative transformation that can have real-world consequences.

Throughout her research, she sought out and listened to a wide range of stories, told primarily by women. Alison's method involved intensive listening punctuated by questions, comments, and affirmations. Her more finished work combines summary and analysis with long passages that allow the interviewees' voices to come through directly. The interviews she had already completed represent a considerable diversity of perspectives on Down syndrome, including those from women who had abortions after a prenatal diagnosis and perspectives from parents of varied faith, class, and racial backgrounds at different stages of parenting. Much of that work is represented here.

With more time, Alison certainly would have thought further not just about the content of these narratives but also about their form. She was already beginning to ask about the affordances of memoir, why stories about the arrival and parenting of children with disabilities share a similar narrative arc, and the consequences of following different paths in telling stories about disability. She might well have spent time identifying the common features of women's stories about prenatal and postnatal diagnoses and parenting children with disabilities. Among her unfinished work was an ongoing reflection on the formal similarities between stories told by women who terminated pregnancies after receiving a prenatal diagnosis and those who chose to continue. In trying to make sense of the accounts she had collected, Alison examined the common narrative devices women use to navigate the bewildering array of decisions around pregnancy, childbirth, and parenting. Eventually, she might also have considered the limits of personal stories as sources of knowledge and meaning. As the literary critic Amy Shuman asks, what are the possibilities and perils of using "other people's stories" as the grounds for empathy and for moral action?[6]

If *story* is one link between Alison's earlier and later visions of her project, the other is *prediction*. Alison's research on prenatal diagnosis asks, in essence, what stories we bring to, and build from, predictive information. Her approach overlaps with queer critics who note the oppressive nature of a futurity organized around the expectation of heterosexual reproduction.[7] Similarly, children with disabilities are often thwarted by predictions of a limited and unproductive future. They are described as "delayed" or "backward" to signal their deviation from the standard pace and developmental trajectory of more typical peers. A prenatal diagnosis may even more dramatically change how we imagine the future, usually by limiting or foreshortening our stories about the person a fetus may become. Alison asks how we understand the meaning of a future child's arrival, whether that information is probabilistic (as in a screening test suggesting Down syndrome) or diagnostically certain (as in amniocentesis confirming the existence of Down syndrome). Even when the information is certain, what do we make of the ensuing uncertainties?

Alison approached the challenge of uncertain temporalities as a research question, but she also faced it in her own life. Despite a screening test suggesting an elevated likelihood that Maybelle had Down syndrome, she declined further testing. As a cancer patient, Alison faced a different kind of futurity, living through shocks and reprieves with every new battery of tests—each of which presented its own impossible mix of certainty and uncertainty, as in a prognosis of six to twelve months. Therefore, she understood the impact of prediction both as a parent and as a patient: *MB, and my head.* It seems likely that Alison's later thoughts about the book's direction were fueled by her life and that a scholarly monograph may have seemed insufficient to her embodied experience of the questions she considered.

* * *

In leaving us her manuscript and notes, Alison joins a group of important thinkers who left unfinished work for friends and colleagues to complete. At one point, Rachel collected a list that included such figures as the poet T. S. Eliot, author Ralph Ellison, and critics F. O. Matthiessen, Michel Foucault, Jacques Derrida, Edward Said, Raymond Williams, and Walter Benjamin. The company becomes more diverse with the inclusion of more recent authors like the poet Gary Fisher and cultural critics Chris Bell, Patricia Yaeger, Barbara Johnson, Lindon Barrett, Linda Singer, and William Hawkeswood.

We take a certain comfort in knowing that the challenges we face as editors have been shared by the editors and collaborators on these earlier projects. In Alison's case, the inclusion of personal narrative presents us with special challenges: even as co-authors, we do not claim to speak *for* Alison; we hope that Alison speaks with our help. We are her assistive technology. In this role, we see a partial parallel with the work of parents who speak for their children—and the same ethical conundrums, the shadings of which are implied by prepositions: speaking *for*, speaking *about*, speaking *over*, speaking *with*. We have tried to speak with

Alison or, rather, to let her speak through us—to preserve as much of her agency, her intentions, as we could. Paradoxically, to do so means alteration: collaborating with Alison requires a sort of editorial séance, a conjuring of the Alison we knew. Imagining her, to imagine whether she would approve of a particular change. Would she want this? Would she say this, and would she say this in this way?

In a short essay on writing, Eudora Welty describes the process of revision as driven by listening: she listens to an inner voice and trusts it to make her changes.[8] As editors, we have taken the same approach, but the voice in our heads is Alison's. Our work on this book is driven and shaped by our friendship with Alison; we have tried to listen to the voice on the page and to the voice we remember. The memory of that voice has been our surest editorial guide: Alison in conversation— her emphatic openness, her political fearlessness, her exuberant curiosity, her warmth and affection, her desire to connect and learn, to bear witness to life at its best and worst. (And, less obviously, to her privacy: Alison's openness as a blogger and speaker belied how fiercely she guarded her own privacy and that of her family. We have honored the lacunae too.)

We first met to discuss our work on this project on a muggy day in New York City. There was so much to say in the time between the arrival of George's train into the city and his return later that afternoon. We walked around Midtown, had lunch in a diner, walked some more, and drank some coffee as we tried to talk through what Alison had left us, what was missing, and what our process should be. At one point, we stopped to take a selfie. Neither of us looks great in the photo: the angle is unflattering, our hair is damp, and the sky behind us is a humid white. But afterward we confessed to each other that we felt Alison there with us, almost expecting that she might appear over our shoulders in the picture. In retrospect, our strong sense of Alison's presence is less a spiritual intimation than it is a sign that the project we were starting would involve ongoing work of reviving, revisiting, and engaging with Alison's desires, intentions, and beliefs. In choosing us to be her collaborators, she ensured that she would be present to us throughout the completion of this book.

Of course, our collaboration with Alison is different from working with a living co-author. Some of our constraints have been absolute. While Alison's handwritten notes sometimes clearly signaled her intentions, at other times we couldn't know for sure. She trusted us to carry the project forward, but trust is not license, so we've preferred a conservative approach. (This is probably the only time the word *conservative* has been publicly associated with Alison.) If we made structural changes, it was to bring like subjects together, rather than to formulate a new argument. If we made sentence edits, they were for clarity and concision, but we erred on the side of preserving Alison's voice.

For this reason, we have favored finished work. Two chapters are built around published academic essays, and when assembling chapters from fragments, we have chosen the most polished pieces—nuggets, not raw ore. Wherever Alison appeared unsure of how to interpret or frame a certain chapter, or when her thinking was still developing, we have chosen what we thought was her best and most representative work. This approach was necessary in chapter 2, which is based on a long-running research project in which Alison conducted extensive interviews with women who either terminated fetuses with Down syndrome or carried them to term. In our view, the best treatment of this material was Alison's article "The Inadequacy of 'Choice': Disability, Feminism, and Reproduction," originally published in *Feminist Studies*. This article forms the basis of chapter 2. (We have also drawn on the transcript of a talk Alison gave at Columbia University on January 27, 2014, at a panel titled "Parenting, Narrative, and Our Genetic Futures.") Though many more interview transcripts remain, the development and exploration of this raw material without Alison, who conceived of the project and conducted the interviews, would have been beyond our mandate.

Because Alison thought about the same subjects in many places and many arenas, it wasn't uncommon for her to write about a topic such as prenatal diagnosis in blog posts, published articles, and interviews, as well as in handwritten notes. Where a passage clearly fit with an existing draft, we spliced it in. At the same time, we have made the invisible repairs customarily made by editors, streamlining sentences, line editing for clarity: where a sentence might be tightened without losing Alison's voice, we did so. (George left in a few more adverbs than he otherwise might have, especially ones like *incredibly*, which expressed Alison's verve and exuberance in life. She was *incredibly* excited to read things, to talk about them with her friends, to speak up about what she believed in. For Rachel, it was about preserving Alison's optimism against her own tendency to see contradictions that complicate and undermine).

Early on, our friend Jordana Mendelson came up with the perfect metaphor for our process: the Japanese art of *kintsugi*, in which a broken vessel is fitted together, made whole again, using adhesive laced with gold. Kintsugi is a paradoxical art: by highlighting the jagged seams of the break, the technique holds wholeness and brokenness in a single artifact. In the same way, our own procedures, from this introduction to our individually authored chapters, footnotes, and occasional explanations in italics, are intended not to conceal but to call attention to the act of assembly.

Jordana's insight began with a story Alison had told on her blog, about a favorite coffee mug. The front of the mug bore a cartoon of Princess Leia, holding a blaster and looking badass. Among her many enthusiasms, Alison was a Star Wars fan, and Princess Leia had special significance for her. (From May 2015: "She was a great example of a tough-talking, competent leader who just happened to be a woman. . . . In both my professional and personal life, I aspire to be more like her."[9]) But in an essay published in the *Charleston City Paper* on June 2, 2016, Alison writes that the cup had fallen and broken:

She was gone, broken into five pieces. Drenched with hot coffee, I started to clean the floor. Several kitchen towels were required. And as I cleaned, I started crying. And I cried. I cried so much that I couldn't breathe. I couldn't stop.

After several minutes, I finally knelt on the floor and softly, carefully, touched Princess Leia's face. Her face is fierce. She holds a blaster, facing to the right but looking to the left, as if she has just noticed someone. On the other side of the cup, it reads "Don't even think about touching my coffee, you stuck-up, half-witted, scruffy-looking nerf-herder!" The nerf-herder quote is from *The Empire Strikes Back* rather than the original *Star Wars*, but that doesn't matter. There Princess Leia was, in my hands, broken but defiant.[10]

Alison explains that her brother has researched kintsugi online and that he and her husband would like to repair the cup. She then meditates on what a repair might mean, reflecting on irreversibility, illness, the body, and care:

I know they would spend far more than it was ever worth to have it put back together, to try and return Princess Leia to that moment before the cup shattered on the kitchen floor.

The point, though, isn't for the coffee cup to be fixed, with its injuries rendered invisible. The point now is to recognize the beauty of the effort to mend what is broken, however imperfectly, however incompletely.

The old Princess Leia is gone, after 12 years and thousands of cups of coffee. My old body is gone as well, the result of age and illness. Neither the cup nor I can be made as good as new, and I won't pretend otherwise.

There is value, though, in the effort—the expensive, difficult striving—to put together what has been broken. To honor what was lost, but also what has been gained. In even the failed repair, to see compassion in the work of both potter and physician.

A few weeks after Alison's column, her repaired Princess Leia cup came back to her: art restorers had set aside the priceless museum artifacts they had been working on to do a rush kintsugi restoration of Alison's mass-produced Star Wars coffee cup. On June 26, Alison announced the completed repair on her blog:

> So many things have been challenging, as you all know.
>
> Okay, the bad news is still the bad news. If you have read this blog, you know my diagnosis.
>
> Today, though, I want to celebrate something wonderful. The Princess Leia coffee cup has been remade.[11]

Alison includes photographs, front and back, of the mended cup. Brian offers a postscript, thanking the craftspeople who did the repair. In retrospect, looking at that blog post, we notice its brevity, the changed proportion of photographs to text, and the postscript from Brian. All were indicators of the progress of Alison's disease, of the exhaustion it brought and her increasing reliance on others to help her express herself.

We cannot think of a better metaphor for our work on this project than Jordana's connection with the art of kintsugi. We are not creating a new product of our own; nor are we attempting to erase the seams between fragments. At the same time, we hope to do justice to the shape and purpose of the original design. Of course, every metaphor has its limits. While the term *kintsugi* is apt for the process of piecing this manuscript together, it also suggests a *restored* whole; the chapters here, by contrast, are present in this form for the first time. This book is a kintsugi of the future, an attempt to piece together what Alison did not have time to complete. It is also a synecdoche for loss, because our assembly only suggests what Alison might have achieved, had she had more time.

* * *

In her last weeks, Alison increasingly relied on others to speak. Emails came from family and friends. Sometimes they arrived dictated and jointly signed, like one from her mother, Kelly Piepmeier: *Alison (via Kelly)*. We find the joint signature meaningful. It invokes care, motherhood, scholarly precision. It suggests that even in the worst things we face, the best of us is revealed; we draw on our histories together and our connections, and our mutual dependence comes to the fore. Another email, answering a query about the project, was sent by Alison's dear and longtime friend Catherine Bush:

> *George,*
> > *This is Catherine again. Alison says, great!*
> > *And of course Alison also says . . .*
> > *love,*
> > *Alison*

* * *

Early in 2013, Rachel sent both George and Alison an email:

> Here's my brainstorm idea: we do a three-way dialogue (for somewhere like DSQ [*Disability Studies Quarterly*]), framed as both a conversation about parenting, writing, and advocacy AND as a formal experiment in disability-inspired writing. Where the traditional essay is one author, one argument developed, we are experimenting with co-authorship and interdependent thought/writing. What do you think?

We did present a panel that year at the American Studies Association, but we did not have time to complete the writing project Rachel had suggested or the others we had hoped to do. In a way, this book has absorbed the impulse. It's a continuation of our conversations, and as such, it suggests a second metaphor for our efforts: the idea of the welcome table that is the basis for chapter 3.

If kintsugi suggests the finished product—the book like a repaired cup, its seams deliberately made visible—the welcome table, a favorite metaphor of Alison's, suggests what we hope to achieve. In its focus on conversation, interchange, and community, it suggests the process that, among other things, includes this book. The welcome table is an image of true community, a place where all are invited to gain sustenance while sitting together. For Alison, it is an image not only of the goal of activism and advocacy but also of the process: being "at the table," as Alison writes, is shorthand for being represented and included. With all this in mind, the welcome table could be another metaphor for this book: a locus of conversation, where everyone is welcome as long as they come in a spirit of generosity and inclusion, where those who knew Alison can recall her presence, and where those who didn't can glimpse the friend we lost. But more than that, we hope that others will take up and continue the work laid out here, that this book will be the beginning of a conversation and not the end.

1

"I Wouldn't Change You If I Could"

Disability as a Form of Human Diversity

What we call disability is perhaps the essential characteristic
of being human.
—Rosemarie Garland-Thomson, *Bioethical Inquiry*

In 2008, at the age of thirty-five, I was pregnant—for the first time in
my life, *intentionally* pregnant. Although I'd had two abortions in previous years because I wasn't ready to be a mother (and had learned the
hard way that the contraceptive failure rates aren't exaggerated), this
time I was willing to give it a try. This was the first time an early pregnancy test wasn't something I stared at in sick horror or relief. Instead, I
was excited about the plus sign, both terrified and thrilled that we were
going to have a baby.

I immediately made an appointment with my nurse practitioner. She
used a Doppler fetal monitor so that I could hear the rapid heartbeat.
There was somebody in there! Because the pregnancy was intentional, I
thought of the fetus as "somebody," not simply a mass of tissue. I remember that during my first abortion, I craned my head so that I could see
the ultrasound they were performing—I wanted to see what the nurse
saw. It was, in fact, a mass of tissue. And of course, at just a few weeks
into the pregnancy, Maybelle was a mass of tissue, too. But she was a
mass of tissue I'd already given an identity.

When the nurse practitioner offered me a nuchal translucency screening, I agreed because that test would allow an early ultrasound. I don't
remember much about our appointment with the genetic counselor that

preceded the test. I don't remember whether it was difficult to give consent. I do remember that we got to see the little curled-up person, fingers in its mouth. I immediately hung the picture up on the refrigerator when I got home, and I called my mom. "Your first grandchild," I said, "is adorable!"

When I got the results of the screening a few days later, it was the end of the workday. I was in my office, surrounded by student papers and stacks of books I hadn't yet read. The counselor called my cell phone. My heart pounded.

"You have a 1-in-148 risk of having a child with Down syndrome," she told me.

"What's it supposed to be?"

"One in 263 would be the expected rate for your age and health."

Tears sprang to my eyes. I found it hard to end the conversation. I immediately called my then husband, Walter, and when he didn't pick up, I called my friend Claire. By this point, I was sobbing.

Claire was calm, although clearly at a loss. What are you supposed to say? She and I knew nothing about Down syndrome. Neither of us knew anything about statistics. She shared that when she was pregnant with her twins, she'd had an amniocentesis, and that if one of her fetuses had had Down syndrome, she would have terminated. She normalized that procedure. Then she and I found our way into the line of conversation that went, "You know, this statistic is still really low. I'm *sure* this baby doesn't have Down syndrome."

She and I both knew that this was what she was supposed to say, and we both knew that it wasn't quite right.

What was I going to do?

The genetic counselor had encouraged me to have an amniocentesis because it would reveal conclusively whether the fetus had Down syndrome. I'd had abortions, so I knew this was a realistic option: I could wait a few weeks for the next test, and then I could terminate the pregnancy. It was just like the procedures I had gone through before.

Except that this time, I had chosen to become pregnant. I'd told all my loved ones that this baby was on the way. I'd begun putting my hands on my abdomen and saying things to the tiny creature growing in there. The pictures from the ultrasound were still on our refrigerator, pictures of the little alien being, reaching out with tiny little alien fingers. This time was different.

That night, I was desperate for a hamburger. I sat at a table in the back of a restaurant, holding hands with Walter and crying in between bites of food. I have no idea how I choked down the burger. What I remember is presenting him with the information from the phone call and asking, "Should we have an amniocentesis?"

And I waited.

It was a fraught moment. I believe I knew what I wanted him to say, but I wasn't going to push or nudge or even give him a clue. I needed to know what his authentic answer was.

He thought. Then he said, "You know, we already love this person. Does it have to pass a test before it gets to be a member of our family?"

I felt a wave of relief. The thought of withholding love for four weeks while I waited for the amniocentesis and the results made me feel physically ill. This is the phenomenon Barbara Katz Rothman calls "the tentative pregnancy" in her book of the same name. She notes that the availability of amniocentesis (and now perhaps other tests, as well) "changes the pregnancy experience." As she puts it, "The possibility of a bad diagnosis casts its shadow back over the early months, and the flow of time in pregnancy itself is changed with mid-pregnancy diagnosis. Most important, the mother's developing relationship with her fetus is affected by this new technology of reproduction."[1] I was experiencing the challenge to my developing relationship with this being, which shifted back and forth from "fetus" to "baby" as I discussed and thought about further testing. If I were to have an abortion, I would have terminated a *fetus*. But the pictures on my refrigerator were pictures of my *baby*, of my parents' new grandchild.

The amniocentesis and chorionic villus sampling technologies that were fairly new when Katz Rothman wrote her book in 1986 are now a far more normalized part of pregnancy. Having an amniocentesis would not have been a radical move at all within the world of middle-class pregnancy in 2008, but it would have meant that my pregnancy would suddenly have been tentative. I felt then and I feel now that if I'd had an amniocentesis and learned that the fetus had Down syndrome, I would have terminated the pregnancy. And I didn't want to be faced with that choice.

I felt that in some ways, I was in an impossible situation: I didn't want to end my pregnancy, to abort this fetus. Nor did I want to have a child with Down syndrome. The only acceptable option to me seemed to be to have this child, and for this child *not* to have Down syndrome. So although I had a moment of clarity that night eating hamburgers—a moment of clarity I returned to often during the pregnancy—much of the time I was assuring myself that the baby *didn't* have Down syndrome.

On my blog, I posted about this conversation and our decision not to pursue further testing, and there were lots of responses. Many people who commented tried to be reassuring by suggesting that we wouldn't have a child with Down syndrome, reflecting what Claire and I had said to each other and what I wanted to hear. They wrote encouraging messages:

The odds are way in your favor.
My mother was married at 32 and then had 8 healthy children. I don't
know why, but she did.
I was born when my mother was 41. Most people think that I'm fairly
normal and I did score 99% on my verbal GRE.
I find the triple screen test in general to be a very poor screening tool.
I've helped with thousands of births and although there are heartbreak-
ing cases, almost all babies are healthy.

They gave me anecdotal evidence: Lots of people have healthy babies at my age. Those tests aren't reliable. You're warned about things that won't happen.

But one mom I had never met posted that she did have a daughter with Down syndrome: "I just wanted to say, while I hope your baby is born as healthy as any baby can be . . . if s/he is born with DS, you will love him/her no less fiercely." I remember having profoundly mixed feelings about that comment, mixed feelings that spoke to my mixed state of mind. While part of me thought, "Oh, no! She said it could happen! She'll jinx us!," another part felt relief, a feeling like "Yeah, I'm sure she's right. We're going to love this person." And I went to her blog several times and looked at pictures of her daughter, Georgia—a beautiful, dark-haired toddler who smiled, reached out to her mother, and fed herself a ham and cheese sandwich. I learned things that made me laugh, like that Georgia's favorite toys came from the recycling bin—why buy dolls when she's playing with an old waffle box? Her mother gave me the beginnings of a different story.

Even with this comment from Georgia's mother, though, throughout the rest of my pregnancy, I continued to feel worry along with satisfaction and hope—often at the same time. I remember that close to my due date, I would calm my anxieties by singing songs to my huge pregnant stomach, deliberately unconditional songs, like the bluegrassy one that goes,

> I wouldn't change you if I could,
> I love you as you are.
> You're all that I would wish for,
> if I wished upon a star.
> An angel sent from heaven,
> you're everything that's good.
> You're perfect just the way you are,
> I wouldn't change you if I could.

This was partly a sweet, comforting lullaby to the not-yet-born baby and partly a deliberate political statement to myself. I was encouraging myself to be open to the possibility that this being inside me was a *person*, not a defect or a burden, and that someone with Down syndrome could be valued and valuable. This idea of acceptance is one reason the comment from Georgia's mother on the blog was so significant. She made a point of visiting blogs like mine and writing reassuring messages, because she understood that most of the comments implied that things will be fine *as long as the child doesn't have Down syndrome*. She wanted to offer another perspective, a story other than the dominant and stereotypical ones our culture perpetuates. She told me that things were going to be fine no matter what.

* * *

I soon discovered that Georgia's mother was not alone. Many mothers of children with Down syndrome abandon familiar narratives about disability because their own children invite them to reimagine human value and to view the world differently. Anthropologist Gail Heidi Landsman, in *Reconstructing Motherhood and Disability in the Age of "Perfect" Babies*, interviewed mothers of children with a variety of disabilities. The mothers described "a personal transformation" in which they started "embracing the very qualities in [their children] that are labeled by society as abnormal. The child's impairment is in this interpretation not relegated exclusively to a biology separate from the self, but rather is understood as integral to the child and infused with meaning."[2] In other words, parents can use their experience as a way to challenge familiar narratives that equate disability with abnormality, alienation, and loss of self.

Scholars and advocates argue that we must address our misunderstandings of disability by changing our social narratives rather than by trying to cure or correct individual differences. Disability studies scholar Simi Linton critiques the way that our society frames disability as "an individual burden and personal tragedy." She argues, "Society, in agreeing to assign medical meaning to *disability*, colludes to keep the issue within the purview of the medical establishment, to keep it a personal matter and 'treat' the condition and the person with the condition rather than 'treating' the social processes and policies that constrict disabled people's lives."[3] Instead of seeing disability as a description of an individual, biological condition, Linton and other disability studies scholars identify disability "as a political category."[4] In her view, cultural stories about disability shape power structures and designate certain people as not fully human. By making disability private rather than public, individualized rather than part of our shared community, our familiar narratives protect able-bodied people from having to see the pervasiveness of disability.

Starting with Georgia's mother, I met many others who were taking on the hard work of changing the narratives about Down syndrome. Almost all these women had initially encountered negative perspectives. They were familiar with the story that their child or potential child was tragic and imperfect, and they had developed tools of resistance—ways of recognizing disability as a form of human diversity. These mothers showed me different ways we can radically reframe human worth. Their approaches differ, but in every case, the mothers' experience of raising their children altered their perceptions of the world in unexpected, complex, and enriching ways.

"The ultimate challenge of this work," Landsman explains of her own research, "is not to determine how what we know about mothers of disabled children can be used to help parents 'adjust' or to 'cope' with children's disability, but rather to imagine how what mothers of disabled children have come to know can be used to further our understanding of humanity and to promote the expression and experience of full lives for all people."[5] Landsman invites us to imagine the world differently, to imagine a fuller conception of personhood. This imaginative transformation is something many mothers of children with Down syndrome have experienced—as I found while talking with mothers whose new understanding of the world had led them to activism. The best known of these mothers is the writer Emily Perl Kingsley.

EMILY PERL KINGSLEY

There's so much value and change in the pride and joy without having to say anything and there are difficulties and challenges without having to say anything.
—Emily Perl Kingsley

Emily Perl Kingsley wrote for *Sesame Street* from 1970 to 2015. Her son Jason was born with Down syndrome in 1974. Her experiences with Jason inspired her to include people with disabilities in the *Sesame Street* cast, such as an actor who uses a wheelchair (Tarah Schaeffer) and even Jason himself. Jason's story was the topic of an hour-long NBC television special in 1977, titled *This Is My Son*. With co-author Mitchell Levitz, Jason wrote the book *Count Us In: Growing Up with Down Syndrome*.

In 1987 Kingsley wrote "Welcome to Holland," a widely published and translated essay comparing the experience of finding out your child has a disability with having a trip to Italy rerouted to Holland. The same year, a made-for-television movie she wrote, *Kids Like These*, premiered on CBS. The film, about a middle-aged couple who have a son with Down syndrome, won numerous awards. Kingsley continues to speak and work as an advocate for people with Down syndrome and other disabilities.

* * *

In the days after Maybelle was born, a friend sent me an essay by Emily Perl Kingsley. Published in 1987 and widely translated since, "Welcome to Holland" equates having a child with Down syndrome to booking a trip to Italy and landing in Holland instead. The journey isn't what you imagined, but it has unexpected pleasures and joys. At the time, I found the essay incredibly helpful because of the way it validated difference—Holland isn't worse than Italy; it's just different.

At the same time, my experience has been very different from Kingsley's. Near the end of the essay, Kingsley writes, "Everyone you know is busy coming and going from Italy . . . and they're all bragging about what a wonderful time they had there."[6] I can see what she means, but this part of her allegory doesn't really fit with my experience raising Maybelle. Yes, my friends with typical kids talk about their achievements, what school they're going to go to, how many friends the kids have. But this talk isn't a way to shut me down or to show off their kids' accomplishments. Kingsley also writes about pain "that will never, ever, ever, ever go away . . . because the loss of that dream is a very very significant loss." Here too my experience has diverged. Not long ago, a friend of Maybelle's said, "I can write my whole name. Why can't Maybelle write her name?" I felt able to acknowledge that her friend is brilliant (at age six, he can read like a third-grader. He speaks beautifully and can express big ideas). But when I compare him with Maybelle, I don't feel that I'm carrying a lifetime of grief.

When I had the chance to meet Emily—visiting her home in New York for a couple of days in 2015—I recognized points of connection and significant differences. There were many moments when I felt that we were exactly aligned ideologically. At other times, I realized I might see a different set of possibilities because pioneers like Emily and her son Jason made these options possible.

* * *

When I met with Emily, she told me about two early experiences that shaped her approach to disability. In each case, her infant son was devalued—once by a pediatrician and once by March of Dimes.

When Jason was born in 1974, Emily and her husband Charles met with a pediatrician. "This person will be taken away," the doctor said. "He will become part of an institution. He's a mongoloid. . . . You can tell your families that the child died at childbirth. You can start again, have a real child." Although they were terrified, Emily told me, they knew that they could not let this child go. Another doctor said, "Try [taking Jason home] for six months." So they did. A few months later, Jason and Emily were photographed by a professional from March of Dimes. "We assumed these photos were just for our family," Emily told me. "And we thought they were beautiful—just beautiful."

Several weeks later, she saw that the pictures were part of a huge poster for March of Dimes on the walls of the subway. Without her knowledge or permission, the organization had attached the caption "Birth defects are forever unless you help!" March of Dimes wasn't demanding services to help families affected by Down syndrome. Instead, it was selling a message of prevention. Emily recalled, "I was flattered MOD wanted to use our photo but had no idea that they wanted to use it for that awful purpose. I guess they do see DS as a 'birth defect.'"

Because Emily was living in a world that told her to institutionalize her son and where organizations like March of Dimes portrayed him as defective, she had to prove that Jason was a valid human being. This was no easy task. It was months before she even met another family with a child with Down syndrome. "It was an absolute wasteland," she told me. "My god, there were no positive role models to look at. I remember some of those books. I mean, I'm not in favor of book burning, but for those books, whoa. They were 'a mongoloid child.' Oh god, I remember some of those books so vividly." Emily describes her experience as a pioneer as "terrifying. It was absolutely terrifying." But for her, it was also a time of exploration. She filled Jason's space with music and colors. She would take him for walks, talking constantly. At four months, he touched the flower on his wall. She took this as a sign that things could change: he was going to be a real person in the world.

During my visit to her home, Emily and I talked about activism. I characterized myself (inaccurately, I saw, as I read the transcripts of our conversations) as being 100 percent activist. In response, Emily said, "I am sort of, I would say ninety percent, but it's still pretty sad a lot of times. And there's only so much you can change. And there are still some pretty sad moments when you see that it's not changing fast enough. . . . The world is not such a beautiful place for them, ultimately. And I don't mean to ruin it for you, but you're giving me carte blanche to say the way it really is." She continued:

> I had to decide whether my son is only worthwhile if he's a superstar. Because what happened with Jason is that he very quickly became a superstar. You know, he was reading earlier than his typical peers. He started reading between three and four. And at age four, he was reading. And we were taking him into schools and saying, "What kind of classes do you have for a kid with Down syndrome who's reading at four?" And they would laugh at us. And they—and they said, "No, that's ridiculous. Kids with Down syndrome don't read at all." They said, "Don't bother teaching academics to these—this kind of kid—kids like these because they can't do it, and they'll never need it, and we don't bother wasting our valuable time teaching academics to these kids because they can't do it."
>
> And then we would take him in there, and he would read stuff off the wall. And, you know, it was ridiculous because he was counting—when he was seven years old, he could count to ten in twelve different languages. I mean it was ridiculous, he was so—he was so ahead of everybody else. He was—you know, he was doing math. He was doing adding and subtracting. He could do fractions. He could do percentages. So I kidded myself into believing that I had this licked, that I had made it go away, that I had beaten it, that this kid was a superstar, and that this was a joke. That, you know, what do you mean, mentally retarded? This is ridiculous. This kid was counting in Hindi. He was counting in Swedish. He was counting in Russian. He was counting in Hebrew, and counting up to ten in twelve different languages. You know, what are you talking retarded?
>
> And then at eight, when he was eight, the whole world caught up and passed him by. Somehow, when he was eight was when everybody got

smarter than him. Everybody caught up. Eight is when the whole rest of the world got very savvy and got very street-smart.

Then he was playing soccer and everybody knew what to do, and he couldn't figure it out at all. He couldn't figure out the strategy. They're all running this way. He's running the other way. You know, he could run. He could kick the ball a country mile, but he couldn't figure out the strategy at all. He didn't know which side was which. He didn't know, you know— and it was a nightmare.

And I had a whole new crash. Because at eight years old is when the whole rest of the world gets very street-smart. That's when they all start playing video games, and they all start, you know, getting into Power Rangers and, you know—it may be earlier now, for all I know. But when we were doing it, it was when everybody was eight years—in second grade. Second grade, the whole rest of the world caught up, and I had this whole second crash.

That's when I realized that I had a kid with a developmental disability. And I crashed something terrible. It was horrible. That's when I realized— and that's when I said, "Hey, wait a minute. Does my kid only—is my kid only worthwhile if he's a superstar? Is it okay to be a plain, ordinary person with Down syndrome, or isn't it? Do you have to be a superstar to be okay in this community, in this society? Or can you be who you are?"

It has to be okay to be who you are, because not everybody's going to be a superstar, and not everybody's going to be able to count in twelve languages. And I had worked so hard to make this kid extraordinary. And then I realized that it was my fault, that I—that the whole thing was my fault. That I had made myself so crazy to make this kid—to make it go away.

It was my story. It wasn't his story. It was my story. And I had worked so hard to make this not true. Not true. And it wasn't true that he had this thing. And I had to wake up and realize that it was true, and that this is who he was, and this is what he had, and I was going to have to live with it for the rest of my life. Boy, I had a horrible time.

The struggles of this period prompted Emily's return to activism. She recognized the power in her new understanding, and she began trying to make changes in Jason's environment rather than prove he could be better than everyone else:

> If he was in his neighborhood school, and there was more of an atmosphere of, you know, "How can we—how can we be more welcoming and more embracing and—and try to work these kids in and nurture what they might be good at?" Then it could be more of a community. And not, you know—not patronizing or condescending or make the kid the water boy on the football team.
>
> I have to say, I get so irritated. People will send me these YouTube videos of these news stories about, like, "Yeah, the water boy on the football team, they allowed him to kick the ball one time." It's like, that is not a happy story. That is a story of segregation.

In the days I spent with Emily, I got to witness her well-known expertise, her ferocity, her willingness to make changes. She often made Maybelle part of that conversation. "She needs intense speech therapy, like three times a week," she told me. "You can get this approved by the state IEP [individualized education program]. You've got to really fight for this."

Emily talked with me about the joys of being Jason's mom. She feels happy about the world her son is part of, a world in which he could be gay or straight or trans. "There's so much value and change in the pride and joy without having to say anything," she told me, "and there are difficulties and challenges without having to say anything."

Jason is almost exactly my age, so he and I grew up in the same world, and my daughter and I benefit from the activist efforts of Jason and Emily. For instance, they pushed to send Jason to college. "We tried and tried and tried to get some colleges here to be receptive to it," Emily told me. "And we just kept being turned down every time we tried. We were turned away over and over and over again." Jason was ultimately able to spend a year in a college program, where he studied specific subjects but also got a broader and more sophisticated view of what could be possible. Today, thanks in part to the efforts of pioneers like Emily and Jason, colleges increasingly include programs for people with intellectual disabilities. I told Jason about one such program at my college and urged him to apply. He shook his head. "I could have gone a long time ago," he said. I realized that the time had passed. Jason and I are in our midforties, and these programs are intended for typical college-aged students. It's Jason's time to have a job, to be an adult.

While Emily experiences moments of sadness when thinking about Jason's life, she also recognizes that she and her son helped change the world for the better. In my own writing and parenting, I've been influenced both by her writing and by *Count Me In*, the book written by Jason and his friend Mitchell Levitz. *Count Me In* is a series of reflections about topics like disability, work, politics, friendship, and sexuality. The thoughts are voiced by Jason and Mitchell and are transcribed and organized by Emily and by Mitchell's mom, Barbara. Their work has been historically significant. It shows people with intellectual disabilities in a different light, as capable of complex thoughts, feelings, desires, and concern for others.

CINDI MAY

I was Jonah. I was absolutely Jonah. [laughs] You know, I
practically had to get eaten by a whale.
—Cindi May

Cindi May is a psychology professor at the College of Charleston, where she has taught since 1999, also conducting research on aging, cognition, and inclusive education for people with disabilities. She has twenty-year-old twins and sixteen-year-old triplets, including Grace, who had Down syndrome. Grace passed away from leukemia in 2006. After Alison's death in 2016, her daughter, Maybelle Biffle-Piepmeier, joined May's family. Maybelle is now in the fifth grade at Nativity School, where she plays on the basketball team, is a regular altar server, and is a whiz at math.

* * *

Shortly after Maybelle was born, I spent time every day crying. Down syndrome was baffling. I didn't know what Maybelle's life would be like or what I could do to make sure she was happy. I've spent most of my life as an activist: efforts at making the world better were part of my childhood and have been central to my adulthood. Yet here I was, holding this child whose existence led not to action but to questions. What was Down syndrome really like? What should I expect? I recognized the stigmas and stereotypes about people with intellectual disabilities, but I didn't know what to do. I didn't know what needed to change.

Less than a month after Maybelle's birth, I received an email from a colleague I'd never met. Cindi May wrote, "We don't know each other well, but I heard of your wonderful baby news through the grapevine. Congratulations on the birth of your daughter Maybelle!! I am so happy for you." Then she wrote, "As you may have heard, my daughter Grace was born with Down syndrome." Immediately after that sentence, she launched into a list of organizations and the active work she's doing, particularly in terms of making schools inclusive. Her email offered exactly what I'd been looking for, and I was eager to meet with her. I remember pushing Maybelle in her stroller to my college, taking her into Cindi's office, and listening while Maybelle breastfed.

Cindi talked and talked, and I soaked in every bit of it. I'd never heard of inclusive education, so Cindi explained. This was the focus of her activism: teaching schools and others about having classrooms where all students are welcome, not automatically shunted into special education. Cindi's daughter Grace was at the center of that work. As Cindi told me,

"The thing that was really overwhelming to me was not so much accepting Grace's disability but it was accepting the fact that it was going to require so much activism to get what she needed."

Only a month after Cindi and I met, Grace died of leukemia. She was three years old. Cindi recounted her anger and confusion as she tried to reconcile her Christian beliefs with what had happened to her daughter:

> I was really mad about losing her. I was really mad at God, to the point where I didn't even know if there was a God. [When He sent me Grace] we were going to change the world and then He took her away from me. And I could not—for the whole time she was in the hospital, I knew she wasn't going to die, because this kid was going to change the world. You know, so everybody else around me was really nervous, but I knew she wasn't going to die. So I felt pretty betrayed. *Betrayed* is a really good word.

Despairing about Grace's death, Cindi prepared to run in a marathon, something she'd never done before:

> When I was running . . . that was really a time for me to kind of think about things and get my anger out. And this will sound a little hokey but this is my story. I was having this conversation with God about how could you possibly send her to me for a mere three, three and a half years, and then take her away? And I realized on the run that that was exactly what happened to the apostles.
>
> And so I thought, you know what? If they could do that, I could probably get off my butt. So I saw Grace in a weird way as my own personal Jesus, if you will. My way of—okay, she brought me to a new path that I felt that God really wanted me to do, and I clearly had a choice to take it or not take it. And there was a piece of me that, because of the pain, just really didn't want to do it anymore. But I really felt like I'd be betraying Grace, you know? I felt like she was up there and she was

saying, "Come on, you know. It's not just me. It's all these other kids. We all need this."

So I know that, at the risk of sounding egocentric, I kind of felt like I was called to do it. Like, that is what a good person does.

In fact, Cindi is self-effacing about her work. She told me, "I feel really like I'm just doing what anybody else would do. . . . There are lots and lots of parents, I think, who have tried way harder than I have to make changes. . . . I don't like it to be attributed to me personally."

As a parent, Cindi had been researching inclusive education to teach Grace to be confident and to communicate with the world. With Grace gone, Cindi stepped forward to begin a job that she had thought was Grace's. Cindi decided to follow the path from advocacy to activism, gearing her efforts toward making the Catholic school system more inclusive. In doing so, she has not been afraid of confrontation. In a letter she wrote, she framed inclusion as a Catholic value:

When Catholic schools reject students with disabilities—even to provide them with "separate but equal" Catholic education—they send a very powerful message to the entire community. The message is this: Yes, parents, you should find value in every life. Yes, families, you should love and nurture and embrace those who are different, those with special needs. But . . . NO, we will not be there to support and educate those children. They do not belong in our schools with our children without disabilities. Despite our message of acceptance and support for all life, we cannot find a way to include students with intellectual disabilities in our regular schools.

In February 2015—years after we first met—Cindi and I visited a Catholic elementary school with which Cindi has worked closely over the years. She and I were eager for Maybelle to begin first grade there in August. We visited and toured the younger classrooms. Cindi knew the first-grade teacher who would work with Maybelle. After we visited, a team of teachers and their assistants from the Catholic school scheduled a full morning in Maybelle's kindergarten class, so they could get to know Maybelle and her situation and see the support she received. They had conversations that day with Maybelle and the head of Maybelle's school.

A week later, I got a phone call from the principal, who told me that Maybelle wasn't a good fit for the school. My daughter needed too much help. Cindi was both devastated and furious. We debriefed in her car, switching between rage and sadness. But despite Cindi's advocacy, the decision was final. Shortly after that, though, Cindi found me another school for Maybelle, a small, welcoming school called Nativity. I'd had two visits to the school, and on my third visit, Patti, the principal, confirmed that Maybelle would be attending.

"She's accepted?" I asked.

"She's accepted," Patti agreed, smiling. "I thought I told you the last time."

"You told me it was ninety-nine point nine percent," I said.

"Well, she's definitely welcome."

I threw my arms in the air in a "woo-hoo!" and then covered my cheeks and mouth, like I needed to suck up and collect the overwhelming happiness I was feeling in that moment.

Like the other activists I profile here, Cindi is willing to do the exhausting, controversial work to help change the world around her. Many parents of kids with Down syndrome feel satisfied when their child is successful. But others can take it to the next level, interested not only in helping their child but also in helping the larger community. Cindi's advocacy for Maybelle was a small part of her activism. Much of that activism is focused on Catholic schools, but her argument for inclusion's benefits applies to all school settings:

By living and learning with children who have disabilities, our typically developing children learn about empathy, reciprocity, patience, and understanding. They learn the genuine value of people who are different. They learn that having a disability does not equate with being unable or less than. They learn these things by living them every day. What better lessons can we convey to our future business leaders, doctors, teachers, policy makers, and parents? These lessons will help students recognize that disabilities are just another form of diversity, that people with disabilities are an important part of the everyday world, and that people with disabilities deserve full and authentic participation in all parts of society. When they encounter disability as adults, they will respond with optimism, respect, and opportunity rather than fear, ignorance, and intolerance.

STEPHANIE MEREDITH

. . . and being afraid, oh, he's going to live with us forever.
And, you know, now my fear is, oh he might move out.
—Stephanie Meredith

Stephanie Meredith is the Lettercase Program/Medical Outreach Director for the University of Kentucky's Human Development Institute. She holds a master's degree and has written or co-written numerous guides on parenting children with Down syndrome. Among these publications are "Understanding a Down Syndrome Diagnosis," "Diagnosis to Delivery: A Pregnant Mother's Guide to DS," "Welcoming a Newborn with Down Syndrome," "Beyond the Genetic Diagnosis: Providing Parents What They Want to Know" (*Pediatrics in Review*, 2016), and "Impact of the Increased Adoption of Prenatal cfDNA Screening on Non-Profit Patient Advocacy Organizations in the United States" (*Prenatal Diagnosis*, 2016). She offers presentations and training nationwide about bridging the gaps between patient advocacy groups and medical professionals.

* * *

When Stephanie Meredith was twenty-three years old, she and her husband learned that their infant, Andy, had Down syndrome. They knew virtually nothing about the condition, and Stephanie was profoundly overwhelmed. But even her approach to fear was practical:

> I think one of the most productive things that we did is I listed out every single fear that I had and I discussed everything with my husband, and that helped—just to vocalize those concerns—and I mean, the concerns ranged from is he going to make it through this NICU [neonatal intensive care unit] stay, to are people going to make fun of him?

She was fortunate to receive support and information right away but was sad to later learn that this was not the case for many parents and that no resources had been developed specifically for expectant parents receiving a prenatal diagnosis. She quickly decided to kick into gear. Much of the published medical material on Down syndrome that went to potential parents was outdated. It heavily focused on the medical model of disability and had little to say about real-life outcomes. Stephanie decided to create a more up-to-date, accurate, and balanced informational booklet for expecting parents who receive a Down syndrome diagnosis prenatally. She began work on the booklet in 2007 and, three years later, received feedback from the Down Syndrome Consensus Group, which included representatives from a wide range of organizations, including the National Society of Genetic Counselors and the National Down Syndrome Society.

The process was not easy. "It's been a labor of love," she told me. "Definitely kind of a grueling experience in some ways." But the importance of the booklet she produced, *Understanding a Down Syndrome Diagnosis*, was immediately recognized. The publication was approved by representatives from all the major medical organizations and national Down syndrome organizations. It was also controversial because it specifically mentioned abortion, touching on long-standing divisions over reproductive freedom in the Down syndrome community. Although (or perhaps because) the booklet waded into these difficult waters, many parents of children with Down syndrome wanted copies both for themselves and to share with advocacy organizations.

At a certain point, Stephanie's biggest problem was keeping up with the expense and effort of distribution. For a time, she took on this responsibility herself. "Right now," she told me in an early conversation, "my husband and I are personally funding [the booklet]—any doctor who wants to request the booklet can get one." She had received a grant from the National Down Syndrome Society and the Joseph P. Kennedy Jr. Foundation, "and we've been very grateful for that to do our 10,000-book distribution. But that ran out. . . . At this point, it's us." I told Stephanie, "That's both incredibly generous and unacceptable."

Stephanie solved her problem by donating the copyright and administration of the book to the Joseph P. Kennedy Jr. Foundation and the Human Development Institute at the University of Kentucky. She is now the Medical Outreach Director for the National Center for Prenatal and Postnatal Resources at the Human Development Institute, where she has a review board to help with her work, which has included revising, translating, and distributing the book as widely as possible. *Understanding a Down Syndrome Diagnosis* is still available at no charge and can now be downloaded at the Lettercase website, hosted by the University of Kentucky. Lettercase, in its own words, offers "a clearinghouse of accurate, balanced, and up-to-date information about various genetic conditions for expectant parents first receiving the news." The site has significantly expanded its offerings: *Understanding a Down Syndrome Diagnosis* is available in ten languages on the site, which also offers a guide for translators and booklets about many aspects of the Down syndrome diagnosis in both Spanish and English. The website's information on other genetic conditions, such as Jacobsen and Turner syndromes, has also been funded by the Kennedy Foundation.

During our interview, Stephanie described the initial experience of her son's diagnosis: "The day after Andy was born, [a caregiver at the hospital] came in with the book *Babies with Down Syndrome*, which was, you know, the most recent publication at the time. And then she showed us a picture of her son on a bike. For us, that was a very normalizing moment, where it was like, okay, if this kid can ride a bike, that suggested an ordinariness to us that was very comforting."

I told Stephanie how important it had been for my mom to read *Understanding a Down Syndrome Diagnosis*, how different it was from the kinds of things I was given when I was in the hospital. Stephanie and I talked about that transition from being a parent to being an activist and advocate, how she became determined to make change in the world. She also told me about how she designed the contents of the book to speak to medical professionals and expecting parents:

> We were able to talk about things like the lower divorce rate for the parents of children with Down syndrome. But then also we talked about the medical conditions. We talked about the different social services and things like that. And every claim I make in there, we use a study to back it up. And that was very intentional so that it would appeal to that audience [of medical professionals]. But then we also included the photos, and the photos were more to tell the story of Down syndrome. And in all of those photos, we very intentionally did not have the subject looking at the camera. And that was to respect the reproductive choices of the patient looking at the material. Because when you don't have a subject looking at the camera, there's less of an emotional engagement so that it gave them the opportunity to look at it in almost a voyeuristic way to see what life is like for people with Down syndrome. And we wanted all the pictures also to be in context. So we actually interviewed all the families and found out the interests of the people—of the individuals in the photos, and they were all taken on location to show them in context.

Understanding a Down Syndrome Diagnosis reflects a pro-information approach—a response to the conflicts that surround the condition. "I just really think we're looking at a collision between disability rights and reproductive rights with the way that the whole prenatal testing conversation has been framed," Stephanie said. "The only solution in the middle is patient information." At the same time, she understands that there are no easy solutions, and she seemed uneasy about the way she's sitting in the middle of what she described as a "widening chasm." Though the booklet was the product of consensus input, she believes that the consensus is dissolving. "On both sides," she told me, "the book was a disruptive technology."

* * *

If Emily Perl Kingsley was part of the first generation to trigger pro-found social change, then Cindi May and Stephanie Meredith are part of the second. Through their lived experiences, research, and continuous efforts, they've taken part in social activism, and they've seen results. Their efforts are essential: understanding what they have done reveals the potential for people with Down syndrome and other intellectual disabilities.

Not all the mothers I interviewed described themselves as activists, but many were taking on the hard work of changing the narratives about Down syndrome. Like Emily, Cindi, and Stephanie, almost all these women had initially encountered negative perspectives. They were familiar with the story that their child or potential child was a tragic and imperfect figure, and many of them had developed tools of resistance— ways of recognizing disability as a form of human diversity. These mothers showed me different ways we can radically reframe human worth. Their lives and worldviews differed significantly, but each had arrived at a similar place of acceptance after undergoing a personal transformation.

Take, for example, Tara, whose adoration of her son, Eon, who has Down syndrome, emerges in part from her devout Mormon faith. She told me, "He was created in the image of God, as we all were. And I truly believe that Eon was fearfully and wonderfully made and that he was designed to be who he is." This description—"fearfully and wonderfully made"—goes far beyond a tolerant resignation to his disability. Tara celebrates her child for his unique identity and for the characteristics that are part of Down syndrome ("the cute little sandal gap in his toes and the blue circles in his eyes"). Such affirmations didn't emerge automatically from her religious perspective; she told me about other people in her church community who view intellectual disability as something that God will "heal." Tara doesn't see Down syndrome as something that should be healed, because she believes her son "was designed to be who he is." She sees him as so beautiful and significant, she told me, that she was a tiny bit disappointed when her next child didn't have Down syndrome, and she and her husband recently adopted another child with the condition.

Other mothers whose lives are dramatically different from Tara's have shared her celebratory view of Down syndrome. Meriah describes herself as "super-supportive of women's rights, including the right to have an abortion if that's what a woman chooses," and she doesn't identify as religious. In an email, she specifically named characteristics associated with Down syndrome as qualities she loves in her daughter, Moxie: "I love her physical mannerisms . . . I love her size. . . . I love her teeth . . . I love the way she looks . . . I love the way her mind works." After each of these headings, Meriah described how these characteristics manifest themselves in Moxie and how and why she loves them. For Meriah, as for Tara, Down syndrome isn't something to mourn or to wish away. As Meriah says, it's part of "the diversity of human existence," one of the things that make the world richer and more interesting. In a recent blog post about scientific experiments that might ultimately "cure" Down syndrome, Meriah wrote, "It's a pretty interesting chromosome. Shouldn't we find out more about it before we just go trying to shut it off?"

Another mother, Elizabeth, laughed with me about her daughter Rosemary's antics, the girl's enthusiasm and refusal to be still. Elizabeth said, "Being with Rosemary has changed my life so profoundly for the positive, that I obviously wouldn't have it any other way. She reaches out and bridges barriers in society that I couldn't bridge myself." She went on to describe her daughter as "unconditionally loving. . . . That touches [the people we encounter], and I am part of it. She's like a little ambassador of goodwill. So we have positive experiences."

Elizabeth, Meriah, and Tara don't want their children to be healed either by God or by science. Love allows these mothers to value their children just as they are, to cherish their bodily and intellectual distinctions. But they also see these characteristics as more broadly significant—even useful. By doing things in a way that differs from what is dictated by our cultural norms—when Rosemary reaches out affectionately to strangers, or when Moxie dances with "very defined, creative moves that come from *her*"—these children aren't wrong or defective. Instead, their differences give their mothers the opportunity to question whether our societal norms are really in everyone's best interest.

* * *

The mothers I've interviewed are on my mind as I parent my own daughter. Maybelle [*aged five at the time of this writing*] has four floppy girl dolls, all hand-me-downs from an older girl she loves. Maybelle named her initial favorite Lela. The rest are "the girls." Lela and the girls. Like a music group. And in fact, that's sort of how they function: in the mornings, we play music, and she sits on the floor with Lela and the girls, and they all dance and dance, bouncing and flopping their arms.

When the music becomes especially inspiring, Maybelle herself has to dance. She grabs my hand, and we clear off the living room floor. Then we fling our bodies around—sort of like Lela and the girls—to Toni Basil's "Mickey" or Deee-Lite's "Groove Is in the Heart." I'm trying to teach Maybelle to move her hips, but being five, she doesn't yet really have hips. So she bends her knees, jumps, and claps her hands, and I keep dancing with her until I work up a sweat. We both sing along—even, I'm embarrassed to admit, when the song is Toby Keith's "Who's Your Daddy?," to which Maybelle knows the entire chorus. She draws out the last "man," just like in the song. I'm raising her as a feminist, of course, but when the music is fun, I can let a little patriarchy slip in.

I'm the kind of mother I wanted to be. Although I hadn't fully envisioned it before Maybelle was born, what I had hoped for most was that my daughter and I would thoroughly enjoy each other. I'm getting to live a sort of motherhood that feels comfortable to me—and to her, too. I knew from the outset that I would ignore some expectations for "appropriate" motherhood: I wasn't that concerned about teaching Maybelle to be a "good girl," which is a category that distorts people. I was eager for her to be a bit of a troublemaker, particularly the kind who challenges injustice when she sees it. I didn't care about beauty and was happy for her to have her own distinctive appearance (and if that means wearing Spiderman swim trunks and a Mary Poppins hat to school, so be it). I was far more concerned with teaching her to express her own sense of the world than with teaching her to follow the rules and be compliant.

And Maybelle is the kind of person I hoped she'd be: happy, loving, curious, and ready to explore. She has her own opinions, which she's learning to communicate. When she's ready for the three millionth playing of the soundtrack to *Joseph and the Amazing Technicolor Dreamcoat*, she'll tell me, "No more 'Mickey.' Shosheph!" Each morning, she tries a sip of my coffee, pronouncing, "Hot coffee! Yummy!" We have the sort of joy and playfulness and connection that I hoped my child and I would have together.

Of course, we also have our challenges. When Maybelle learned the significance of the word *no*, it became a central part of her vocabulary. She occasionally stands up in the tub and announces, "Pooped in the bath!"—and she's not kidding. She also does some experimenting, like seeing what happens when she drops a glass onto the tile floor, or how many different breakfasts I'll prepare for her in one morning. She astonished me when she carried the kitchen stool to the front door so that she could reach the hook-and-eye lock I'd installed to keep it shut. I've been surprised by some of the things I've yelled at my daughter, but only until I think back to things my mother yelled at my brothers and me. Parenting is, as many people note, not for the faint of heart. The difficult parts of raising Maybelle aren't the fact that she requires occupational and speech therapies. Teaching her sign language in her early years so that she could communicate more effectively wasn't agonizing—it was fun. Using a treadmill to help her learn to walk felt like a sort of adventure. It's *parenting* that's difficult, not the specifics of parenting a child with Down syndrome.

When I learned that Maybelle had Down syndrome, I had the momentary terror—familiar to almost all parents of children with Down syndrome—that this kind of happy life would not be possible and that I would be the most unimaginable kind of bad mother: I would not be able to love my own daughter. I feared that I wouldn't love her, even as I couldn't possibly hold her tighter.

When Maybelle was in her infancy, I latched on to counterarguments that suggested she wasn't deficient, but was simply delayed. As Michael Bérubé explains in *Life as We Know It*, "There's . . . a difference between calling people 'retarded' and calling them 'delayed.' These words may appear to mean the same damn thing when you look them up in Webster's, but I remember full well from my days as an American male adolescent that I never taunted my peers by calling them 'delayed.' . . . A retarded person is just a retard. But *delayed* persons will get where they're going eventually, if you'll only have some patience with them."[7]

I often returned to Bérubé's explanation, and I gave away many copies of his book both to friends who had children with Down syndrome and to those who didn't. Maybelle's physical therapist, who started visiting us when Maybelle was just a few months old, echoed Bérubé's point. She told me at our first meeting—when I was still a bit weepy and quite anxious—that Maybelle would do everything a typical kid would do. She would just do it a bit more slowly, and we'd have to work with her a little more to help her.

I remember how important these concepts were to me, as were the meetings with an activist friend who showed me that Maybelle would be able to read, to talk, and eventually to go to college. These early messages were crucial, helping me ground myself in the basic idea that *everything is just fine.*

But I've begun to move beyond this initial notion that everything is fine because Maybelle's differences are merely delays. The point isn't that Maybelle is as smart as typical folks. The point isn't that she'll *eventually* be that smart, or close to it, if we wait long enough and work hard enough. Nor is the point that she has other qualities that "make up for" her intellectual disability. What would such an idea even mean?

The point is that she's a valuable human being just as she is. Everything is fine because she's a person in the world. I don't want to make her fit into existing systems—I want her to help challenge and change those systems. "Normal" is not the goal. Maybelle may never do certain things our culture defines as normal and therefore acceptable. She may never write, because fine motor skills are incredibly difficult for her. Even at five, she hates holding a marker and will only make vertical lines and circles on the paper. She's an impressive reader, at this point more literate than many of her classmates, but this is in large part because people with Down syndrome are often visual learners. It doesn't mean that Maybelle is "smarter." Will she ever talk clearly? Will she ever understand mathematics enough to pay for things? Will she ever be able to drive? I don't know.

And yet I argue that she's a full and valuable person, nonetheless. This recognition begins with me and with my family, but it doesn't stop there. It demands broader societal recognition, both at the practical level—with inclusive schools, therapeutic supports, accessible housing, and all the rest—and at the ideological level, in the ways we evaluate human identity.

It's often an intimate connection of love or friendship that allows someone to see beyond popular, stigmatizing narratives about disability. I may have believed that someone with an intellectual disability was a tragic figure, but my intimate connection with Maybelle demonstrates to me experientially, kinesthetically, emotionally—and ultimately even cognitively—that my previous views were bullshit. Maybelle is a joy. Her morning dancing, her happy proclamations of "Good morning!" to strangers as we bike to school, her arm-waving excitement when she sees her Uncle Trey, are all great pleasures in my life. Although she is also a child and thus creates plenty of challenges, to see her as tragic, as better off having been prevented from being in the world, is a harmfully limited view—harmful to Maybelle, to me, and to the culture perpetuating tragic stories.

Over time, populations that have been dehumanized have demanded that their culture assess human value differently, and ultimately the culture began to shift. When I published an essay about Maybelle in the *New York Times*, one reader responded to the negative comments: "I refuse to believe the Times would be allowing 90 percent of these comments if we substituted the words Down Syndrome with 'poor' or 'black.'" In other words, since we recognize impoverished people or people of color as fully human, we must do the same for people with disabilities. I'm not saying that people with disabilities are in some easy way equivalent to people of color, women, or impoverished individuals (in part because many people with disabilities *are* people of color, women, or impoverished, or some mix of these qualities—it's not an either-or situation). But our understanding of personhood *can* change, and it should.

To ask what Maybelle contributes, what she's worth, is the wrong question. Instead we should ask what would happen if we began recognizing people with disabilities as fully human. Making space for a broader range of acceptable people is a healthy impulse, one that incites individual and societal transformations. It has made our society *better* not to have to cultivate and maintain a logic that excludes. When we don't have to create strict—and arbitrary—boundaries that determine who belongs, we become a more just, admirable community. Expanding our definition of personhood, of humanity, expands each of our lives. *No one should have to pass a test to be human, to be part of a community, to be loved.* We all benefit from inclusion and from changing the community so that it accommodates all of us.

2

The Inadequacy of "Choice"

Disability, Feminism, and Reproduction

In March 2012, I published an article about abortion and disability on the *Motherlode* blog of the *New York Times*:[1]

I support abortion rights. I've had two abortions. I've body-blocked protesters trying to stand in the way of women entering a women's health clinic that provides abortions. I teach about reproductive rights in classes. I have a bumper sticker advocating abortion rights. I've written about abortion and gotten hundreds of e-mails, many of them angry in tone, from those who disagree with me.

I also have a daughter with Down syndrome—and apparently, that's not how abortion-rights campaigners are expected to play the game.

When I was pregnant with Maybelle four years ago, we learned we had a higher-than-average chance of having a child with Down syndrome. My partner and I wanted to have a child, and we decided we weren't doing any more prenatal testing. Whatever potential person I was pregnant with was going to be part of our family, no matter what.

Many women facing similar news get additional tests. Last fall, a new maternal blood test was introduced which, unlike chorionic villus sampling (CVS) or amniocentesis, offers genetic information about the fetus with no risk of miscarriage. A second test came on the market this week. Media coverage has referred to these tests, and others like them in development, as "the holy grail of prenatal testing" and "a game changer."

These new tests are marketed for their effectiveness at identifying Down syndrome. And if prenatal testing shows that a fetus has Down syndrome, up to 92 percent of them are terminated.

Ninety-two percent. Why is this rate so high?

In addition to being a parent and a reproductive rights advocate, I am also a scholar. I want to know the answer to this question: How do potential parents approach the issue of prenatal testing, and how do they make their decisions? I'm now interviewing what one friend calls "the 8 percenters," parents of children with Down syndrome, and what I've found is that we're not all who politicians like Rick Santorum think we are.

Reproductive decision-making is far more complex than easy sound bites suggest. Many of the women I've interviewed are emphatically supportive of reproductive rights, and have had abortions in the past. When they were ready to have children, they chose to go ahead with pregnancies even after the Down syndrome was identified. And they're happy with that decision.

The complexity has a flip side: women like Emily Rapp, who recently reflected, in *Slate*, on the contradiction between her passionate love for her son, who has Tay-Sachs disease, and her belief that it would have been "an act of love" to abort him—as she says she would have, if her prenatal testing had revealed his condition. She explains, "That it is possible to hold this paradox as part of my daily reality points to the reductive and narrow-minded nature of Rick Santorum's assertions that prenatal testing increases the number of abortions."

"The bottom line is that a lot of prenatal tests are done to identify deformities in utero and the customary procedure is to encourage abortions," Mr. Santorum said during an appearance on CBS's *Face the Nation*.

Unfortunately, in one sense, he's right. The message that sometimes accompanies positive prenatal testing for Down syndrome is: "You have a defective fetus. Let's get rid of it so you can try again." One mother I interviewed was told by her obstetrician, "The quickest, cheapest way to solve this problem is to terminate the pregnancy."

But that doesn't have to be the case. The prenatal testing is not what we should question, but the assumptions that accompany it. I agree with Ms. Rapp's call for "a more nuanced discussion." All disabilities are not the same. If our culture assumes that across the board, a child with a disability is defective, and a problem best avoided, then we're encouraging people who want to be parents to make a decision based on bad information. And having an abortion because of bad information is a preventable tragedy.

I was terrified when we learned that Maybelle has Down syndrome, terrified that she would never walk or talk, that I would have to quit my job, that I would not be able to love her. Ultimately, I was terrified that she was, in fact, "defective," and that she would not be a whole human being.

What I needed at that point wasn't more restricted access to prenatal testing. It was better access to accurate information about what I could expect as the parent of a child with this particular disability. My fears were based in stereotypes about Down syndrome and disability more broadly, and they were simply wrong.

Abortion is an incredibly important option for people who are not ready to be parents. I had abortions when I wasn't ready for a child in my life. Those pregnancies were accidental, and I'm grateful to have had access to abortion. I had Maybelle intentionally, prenatal testing and all, and I'm grateful for that.

The article received over 170 online comments. Given that the paper is aimed at a thoughtful audience, many of whom identify as liberal, it wasn't surprising that many readers accepted abortion as an available option for pregnant women. What did surprise me was the eugenicist use to which many of these readers would put abortion. They offered the choice of abortion as a way to avoid what they saw as an unacceptable situation: having a child with a disability. Here are several of the comments:

> A condition that brings with it guaranteed cognitive disabilities is not something I'm willing to inflict on another human being, much less my own beloved child.
>
> Knowingly giving birth to a special needs child is a crime against the child.
>
> I resent having to pay for children who are going to be a huge drain on society, financially and resource wise, if the parents knew in advance that they were going to have a special needs child.
>
> I was raised to believe that knowingly giving birth to a severely disabled or mentally retarded baby was a sin—a really terrible sin—because it harmed not just the baby (who would never have a normal life) but also the family (including siblings who would be pressed into caring for an aging disabled brother or sister, no longer "cute" in their 50s) and society (stuck with enormous bills for a lifetime). I still feel that way. Hopefully in time, that 92% [of fetuses with Down syndrome that are terminated] will become 100%.

While the comments as a whole were diverse, responses like these were not rare. They are examples of the troubling narratives that surround reproduction, disability, and parenting in our culture. Readers described giving birth to a person with a disability as an act of "harm" or cruelty, even as a "crime," deeply stereotypical framings that individuals with disabilities and their supporters might well dispute. People with disabilities were being defined principally as "a huge drain on society." The term "normal life" was used as though it were an unambiguous goal, without acknowledging the extent to which this narrowly imagined construct fails to embrace the diversity of human existence. The final comment concludes with the clearly eugenicist hope that 100 percent of fetuses with

Down syndrome will be terminated. The world, presumably, is a better place if people with Down syndrome or intellectual disabilities aren't in it.

Even more striking in these comments, both positive and negative, was the rhetoric that framed reproduction in terms of choice. Among those who supported the decision to continue a pregnancy after a diagnosis of Down syndrome were readers who wrote these comments:

> Now, regardless of my stance regarding abortion/choice, what am I to think of those who believe my son, who was diagnosed with Down syndrome at birth, is not fit to exist?
>
> As the staunchly pro-choice mother of a daughter with a rare genetic syndrome, one thing that I know for sure is that it would have been the biggest mistake of my life to have terminated my pregnancy had I known about her condition.
>
> This is a great article. I, too, am strongly pro-choice and have a son with Down syndrome. I didn't do prenatal testing, because I felt (and feel) that the things I was most afraid of were not things I could test for: rapist, murderer, right-wing radio host who calls young and intelligent women "sluts."

The vocabulary of choice was just as prominent among those who opposed my argument. For example, one reader responded, "For me, the choice to abort would have been simple. Fortunately, I didn't have to make that choice. It is not easy, but for me, it would have been the only choice." So too, this vocabulary ran through the comments of those who wanted to emphasize the importance of reproductive rights, regardless of the decisions made by individual women:

> I do feel that the choice for others should be available in regards to imperfections in the birth. This is not saying you keep throwing back the ones you don't want but merely have the choice to accept a down baby or not.

We should all be thankful that people have a choice. That the govern-
ment doesn't force abortions on fetuses with birth defects and allows
the 92% to terminate when necessary. No matter what our position,
we should all fight for the right to choose.

We made our choice but I can really understand how someone else (or
even us at a different point in our lives) would not have felt able to
continue with this pregnancy.

Although I am 100% pro-choice (and had an abortion when I was a
teenager) I realized that I would never have terminated a DS baby. I
respect both choices—to terminate, or not, but know what my choice
would have been.[2]

Perhaps the charged position of choice in this feedback was unsurprising, given that the editor had titled my essay "Choosing to Have
a Child with Down Syndrome." More striking, however, is the way it
echoes published feminist writing, which also frames the conversation about reproductive rights in terms of choice while relying—albeit
in more nuanced ways—on uncritical stereotypes about disability. The
fact is, most feminist conversations haven't gone beyond the level of this
online commentary. They are limited not just by feminist understandings of disability, but by feminist framings of reproduction. In short,
the narrative of choice that surrounds and defines the discourse on US
reproductive rights is simply inadequate.

During my pregnancy, when my partner and I were deciding whether
to have an amniocentesis and, presumably, an abortion if the fetus had
Down syndrome, I discovered that feminist texts had little to offer me.
My story isn't one that many feminists are talking about—or if they are
talking about it, they are doing so in ways that I found troubling rather
than helpful. The feminist writing I have in mind relies on a number of
reductive and stereotypical narratives about reproduction and disability.
These problematic narratives are particularly visible in (rare) feminist
discussions of prenatal testing and abortion. Such discussions are often

built around stereotypes of people with disabilities, of parenting people who have disabilities, and of what *choice* means.

This criticism is not merely a semantic quibble. Feminist conversations about disability and abortion suggest broader problems within feminist discussions of reproduction. In what follows, I'll argue that reproduction should not be defined by choice, a concept that emphasizes the individual at the expense of broader societal contexts that shape reproduction, parenting, and our understanding of children. For feminist scholars to address reproduction in a meaningful way, they must resist stereotypes that perpetuate oppression. They must instead listen to a different set of narratives, those told by pregnant women and by parents of children with disabilities. We need scholarly and activist feminist conversations that embrace, rather than fear, the complexity of reproductive decision-making.

My research project emerged partly from my desire to hear the stories of other individuals' decision-making. I've conducted a series of interviews with pregnant women and with parents of children with Down syndrome. From these conversations, I've learned that reproductive decision-making is far more complex than what mainstream feminist narratives suggest. Prenatal testing and selective abortion were the starting point for the conversations, but this isn't an argument exclusively about prenatal testing, Down syndrome, or genetic disability. The narratives emerging from decisions about whether to have prenatal testing and whether to terminate a fetus can serve as case studies for ways that feminist discourse around reproduction needs to change.

This chapter will present examples from both popular and scholarly writing to illustrate the limitations of feminist conversations around disability and reproduction. Narrowly focused on the importance of choice, these conversations oversimplify reproductive decision-making by focusing on individual women and drawing uncritically on stereotypes about disability. The chapter will then show how such perspectives are complicated by the narratives of the actual parents and pregnant women who were my interview subjects. Finally, I'll turn to reproductive justice discussions that offer a scholarly counterpart to the stories of reproductive decision-making gathered in my interviews.

Feminist Narratives

The gap between the agendas of feminist advocates of reproductive rights and those of disability rights has been problematic for some time. Commonly framed in terms of choice, reproductive freedom has been a cornerstone of the modern feminist movement, which holds that women cannot be equal citizens without the right to abortion. The feminist position emphasizes the woman's interests—her right to choose—over those of the fetus. Often, the severely disabled fetus has been used (along with the health of the mother) as a limit case in the argument that abortion must remain legal, and majority public opinion has consistently supported abortion for these reasons.[3] Many advocates of disability rights also support reproductive freedom while wanting to draw an ethical, if not a legal, line at selective abortion, that is, the termination of an otherwise wanted pregnancy because of a diagnosis of disability. Focusing their attention on the disabled fetus, they argue that selective abortion is part of a broader cultural devaluation of people with disabilities.

Some feminist literature attempts to affirm the dignity and autonomy of both pregnant women and people with disabilities. As early as 1984, Marsha Saxton was writing as a feminist who supports reproductive rights and who "question[s] the practice of systematically ending the life of a fetus because it is disabled."[4] Her rhetoric indicates the difficulty of this position: *fetus* is the preferred term among advocates of abortion because it implies a stage prior to independent life, emphasizing the needs and desires of the pregnant woman who carries it. However, Saxton also refers to the fetus as having a "life," language often used in anti-abortion arguments, which hold the fetus to have rights distinct from those of the pregnant woman. In 1998, Saxton more thoroughly articulated the divide within reproductive politics, calling for an alliance between those who gave priority to the rights of women and those who supported people with disabilities: "The reproductive rights movement emphasizes the right to have an abortion; the disability rights movement, the right not to have to have an abortion. . . . We must actively pursue close connections between reproductive rights groups and disabled women's groups with the long-range goal of uniting our communities."[5] Despite Saxton's call for closer connections, the divide between these groups has been widened by the advent of cheaper and less invasive prenatal tests that allow pregnant women to know earlier whether the fetus they are carrying has a genetic disability.

Saxton's call for unity came in a decade marked by the emergence of such major feminist disability publications as Rosemarie Garland-Thomson's *Extraordinary Bodies: Figuring Physical Disability in American Literature and Culture* (1996), Susan Wendell's *Rejected Body: Feminist Philosophical Reflections on Disability* (1996), and Nancy Mairs's *Waist High in the World: A Life Among the Disabled* (1996). These books challenged the common view of disability as a personal misfortune. They reframed it as a form of human diversity that should be accommodated and, in some cases, even celebrated. Yet despite the counternarratives made available by a growing body of feminist disability scholarship, popular feminist writing continued to reinforce problematic attitudes toward disability.

The introduction to an edited collection titled *Choice: True Stories of Birth, Contraception, Infertility, Adoption, Single Parenthood, & Abortion* (2007) shows how those attitudes are a by-product of the discourse of choice. Editors Karen Bender and Nina de Gramont offer a range of ideas for promoting reproductive freedom, including such common strategies as making sex education more widely available and including contraception on health-care plans. They also offer the following suggestion: "Instead of banning late-term abortions, why not create a test for genetic abnormalities that will detect problems earlier in pregnancies, so that women can learn about the health of their fetus earlier and make the choice that is right for them?"[6] They present early testing as common ground, suggesting that the controversy over abortion hinges on when in the pregnancy the procedure takes place. Differences of opinion would dissipate, they propose, if fetuses with disabilities could be terminated in the first trimester.

Notice that their reframing affirms the possibility that parents could "make the choice" earlier, implying a tacit understanding that abortion would be among those choices. Imagine how different their account would be if they argued for understanding the potential personhood of a fetus with "genetic abnormalities" as other than defective goods. In what is overall a thoughtful, nuanced book on reproduction, the editors reinforce stereotypical thinking about prenatal testing and disability—viewpoints that influence the broader feminist conversation about reproduction. When they were editing this book, the new, noninvasive prenatal tests did not exist, but as these tests entered the market, their existence would trigger the very conversations about prenatal testing that the editors in this collection seem not to anticipate.[7]

Bender and de Gramont follow a familiar strategy in positioning choice as the end point rather than the beginning of further discussion. The difficult decisions arising from unwanted results are presumably left to individual women. Naomi Wolf's *Misconceptions: Truth, Lies, and the Unexpected on the Journey to Motherhood* (2001) and Amy Richards's *Opting In: Having a Child without Losing Yourself* (2008) are popular feminist tracts that go further by imagining what their authors would do if faced with unwelcome news. Both thoughtful books use the author's personal experience of pregnancy to frame a larger feminist conversation about reproduction and motherhood. Seemingly unaware of feminist disability studies, both authors also make the troubling point that parenting a child with a disability would be a kind of martyrdom that they couldn't tolerate.[8] In doing so, they uncritically employ the same stereotypical views that parenting a child with a disability would involve suffering and sacrifice and that children with disabilities aren't fully human.

Wolf, a best-selling feminist journalist, is known for connecting her personal experience to broader social and political insights. *Misconceptions* uses the story of her own first pregnancy to examine the modern understanding of pregnancy and childbirth. In a brief discussion of prenatal testing, Wolf shares her own results from an early screening:

> When my husband and I got our abnormal AFP [alpha-fetoprotein] test, I was paralyzed with fear and indecision. Like women everywhere, I prayed. I respected and admired women who could give their lives over to caring for a severely disabled child, but I knew I could not do it myself. In an obsessive mental video of caring for such a child, I watched the things I loved in my life be stripped away; I witnessed vivid scenes detailing the exact nature of my own callowness.[9]

Wolf is certainly entitled to confess her fear of parenting a disabled child, but she fails to acknowledge that it is based on inaccurate stereotypes. While she often describes how cultural misperceptions shape the understanding and treatment of pregnancy, Wolf doesn't recognize that her "obsessive mental video" is created by a culture with skewed, dehumanizing views of disability. And although this episode is framed as a self-critical recognition of her "own callowness," she offers no alternative to the view that parenting a disabled child is all-consuming and life-draining. Without such alternatives, readers can only feel relieved when Wolf reveals that her fetus has no disabilities.

Richards, another influential feminist thinker, writes the Ask Amy column for Feminist.com and has consulted for Gloria Steinem and Anna Deavere Smith. She has also written for such publications as *The Nation*, the *Los Angeles Times*, and *Ms.* and co-authored the guidebooks *Manifesta: Young Women, Feminism, and the Future* (2000) and *Grass-*

roots: A Field Guide for Feminist Activism (2004). Combining memoir with more general advice, *Opting In* addresses a range of contemporary women's problems from a feminist perspective, including the biological clock, the working mother, female friendship, and giving birth. The story of Richards's own pregnancy, birth, and early motherhood is woven throughout. During her pregnancy, she didn't receive any results that worried her. But Richards describes her thinking around testing much as Wolf does:

> I opted for the tests, and while I would like to think that I was open to any result, in reality I most likely would have terminated the pregnancy if there was a strong likelihood of a fetal abnormality. I could argue that I was doing this "for the baby's sake," not wanting "it" to be challenged from the get-go, but the truth is that I didn't want the hardship of parenting a child with serious health issues.[10]

Anticipating negative reactions like the responses to my *Motherlode* essay, both Wolf and Richards characterize parenting a child with a disability as a "hardship" requiring them to "give their lives over." Even more dramatically, Wolf fears losing "the things I loved in my life" without any acknowledgment of a corresponding gain. While such fear is understandable given the inadequate information about parenting a child with a disability available in mainstream media and even in medical settings, I am troubled by Wolf's and Richards's failure to investigate their fears.[11] It is as if they had no curiosity about whether their fears were even accurate. They are understandably voicing a feminist resistance to the notion that women should be martyrs to parenthood, but they fail to recognize how stereotypes about disability are affecting their interpretations. Books that were addressed to large readerships—some of them feminist, some of them not—bolster negative stereotypes by failing to examine their fear-based depictions of parenting critically.

Neither Wolf nor Richards can envision herself parenting a disabled child. Although each imagines that doing so would be wrenching, she is certain that she would choose to abort a pregnancy after learning of a positive diagnosis. Similarly problematic narratives appear in scholarly texts addressing prenatal testing. In 1986, sociologist Barbara Katz Rothman wrote the groundbreaking book *The Tentative Pregnancy: How Amniocentesis Changes the Experience of Motherhood*. Although Katz Rothman effectively critiques the notion of choice by detailing the many constraints that guide women's reproductive decisions, she replicates a number of stereotypes about disability, including the idea of mothers as victims and of Down syndrome as a misfortune. She discusses how painful this individualized choice is: "In choosing between the tragedy of a disabled, defective, damaged, hurt, 'in-valid' child, and the tragedy of aborting a wanted pregnancy, a woman becomes responsible for the tragedy of her choice." Later in the same chapter, she notes, "While the abortion calls forth pain and grief, so too does the experience of mothering a child with Downs Syndrome [*sic*]."[12] Katz Rothman describes prenatal testing as a Hobson's choice: there are no good options. This framing of Down syndrome as a tragedy, one that automatically "calls forth pain and grief," is echoed in the comments to my article on *Motherlode*.

Elsewhere in *The Tentative Pregnancy*, Katz Rothman connects Down syndrome to tragedy. Earlier in the book, she offers a nearly two-page description by the sister-in-law of an adult with Down syndrome. The heartbreaking tale concludes: "There is no solution to this sort of retardation other than prevention." The narrator sees cognitive disability as so horrifying that she recommends a nationwide mandate of amniocentesis followed by the abortion of any fetus diagnosed with Down syndrome. Katz Rothman attempts balance by offering the stories of two women who have children with Down syndrome and who describe them as "a complete joy." Although she notes that "neither was unwilling to accept another Downs Syndrome [*sic*] child," these two women are not quoted at length, and their more positive perspective on disability is muted by the extreme negativity of other examples.[13]

Dena S. Davis is a feminist bioethicist whose book *Genetic Dilemmas: Reproductive Technology, Parental Choices, and Children's Futures* claims to give a "fresh look" at prenatal testing. Putting prenatal testing into a social context, she addresses how certain disabilities gain meaning because of available testing:

> For the woman who would not contemplate abortion, or for whom Down syndrome is one acceptable (if not desirable) outcome of pregnancy, the existence of this technology can be oppressive. Women speak of the "rituals" and routines of genetic testing within pregnancy, and of the real difficulty they experience in fighting the momentum of those routines and assumptions if they decide that testing is not right for them. Now that the choice exists whether or not to have a baby with, for example, Down syndrome, the decision to go ahead and have that baby may actually be much harder to make.[14]

In other words, Davis observes that the availability of a test for Down syndrome can change the meaning of the condition. Inaccurately calling Down syndrome a "disease," Davis writes, "Indeed, as testing becomes more and more routine, the disease being tested for becomes ever more dreaded, ever more unthinkable."[15] With this observation, Davis acknowledges the social construction of disability. Having the test isn't neutral; it can create and contribute to fear simply by being offered.

At the same time, some of Davis's core arguments are quite troubling. Her book emphasizes how children and potential children are affected by parents' choices. Ultimately, she concludes that parents who have a child with a disability decide deliberately "to substantively constrain the ability of their children to make a wide variety of life choices when they become adults."[16] It is, she suggests, irresponsible to have a child with a disability, since disability necessarily limits an individual's life choices.

Davis's perception that disabled lives are inherently limited is striking, given that she understands many other challenges that arise from a child's societal circumstances. For instance, she refrains from criticizing parents in disadvantaged minority groups who have children under less-than-optimal conditions because of societal injustice. In such cases, Davis directs her criticism at oppressive social structures that constrain the future of the minority children who are marginalized.[17] Given such acknowledgments, Davis notably does not consider people with disabilities members of an "oppressed minority group."

Scholars had been making compelling arguments about the social construction of disability for nearly two decades when Davis's book was published. In her foundational essay, "Integrating Disability, Transforming Feminist Theory," disability studies scholar Rosemarie Garland-Thomson explicitly compares our understanding of race and gender to that of disability: "Disability is a pervasive cultural system that stigmatizes certain kinds of bodily variations. . . . The informing premise of feminist disability theory is that disability, like femaleness, is not a natural state of corporeal inferiority, inadequacy, excess, or a stroke of misfortune. Rather, disability is a culturally fabricated narrative of the body, similar to what we understand as the fictions of race and gender."[18] Like Garland-Thomson, Davis understands that race is a socially constructed category, "a culturally fabricated narrative of the body," but sees disability as far more biologically grounded and stable in its meaning. She lacks a feminist skepticism for narratives of bodily inferiority, accepting the stereotypes of disability and bodily deviance as accurate.

The writings of Wolf, Richards, Bender and de Gramont, Davis, and Katz Rothman allow a glimpse at some of the problems in feminist views of prenatal testing and disability. My discussion of these texts is meant not to constitute a literature review, but rather to sample the kinds of arguments that continue to trouble discussions of disability and reproductive rights. These works fall short in the way they represent disability as a tragic burden, in their narrow focus on the rights-bearing individual, and in their failure to recognize parenting as embedded in social communities. To find different perspectives, I talked to parents and potential parents. Their stories help make sense of the difficult and unexpected in individual experiences of parenthood, but they also embed those experiences within broader networks of family, community, and society. "The cultural activity of rewriting life stories and kinship narratives around the fact of disability," write anthropologists Faye Ginsburg and Rayna Rapp, "not only provides a model for the body politic as a whole but also helps to constitute a broader understanding of citizenship in which disability rights are understood as civil rights."[19] It is to those life stories that I now turn in search of a more satisfying engagement between reproductive autonomy and the rights of people with disabilities.

Parental Stories

In the summer of 2011, I began interviewing parents of children with Down syndrome, having conversations with them about their pregnancies, their prenatal testing, and their families. Each of these semistructured, qualitative interviews lasted between one and three hours. Because I am interested in the accounts of these individuals' reproductive decision-making, our interviews were intended to be "conversations with a purpose." Although I went into every interview with a list of questions, I discovered that I only had to ask one: "Did you have prenatal testing when you were pregnant?" Almost every conversation has taken off from that single prompt, requiring me to provide very little encouragement.

In searching for parents of children with genetic disabilities to interview, I primarily advertised among local and national Down syndrome organizations. The invitation stated, "I'm interested in talking with parents who decided to have prenatal testing as well as those who decided not to." I interviewed twenty-nine parents of children with Down syndrome. I met with fifteen of these individuals in the Charleston, South

Carolina, area, and all these interviews were conducted in the parents' homes, as was their preference. I conducted phone interviews with fourteen additional people in Vermont, Connecticut, New York, Maryland, Georgia, Ohio, Missouri, Utah, and California.[20]

I also interviewed seven women who were pregnant at the time of the interviews, asking them what tests they were considering (or had undergone), why they were considering (or had chosen) them, and what they planned to do with the results. These pregnant women weren't the population I was seeking out; each of them had contacted me when she learned about the research project and had asked if she could take part.

All the participants I spoke with signed an informed consent document explaining that their participation was completely voluntary, and they could stop the interview at any time. In addition, at the beginning of each interview, I reminded the participants that they could stop the conversation, refuse to answer any question, change their minds about being interviewed at all, ask me any questions they wanted, or suggest a new direction for the conversation.[21] The vast majority of the people I met with were white, although I sought out women of color and talked with four African American women.[22] Virtually all the participants were middle class, a particularly significant variable since it meant that they had access to prenatal medical care and to second-trimester abortion services, even if those services would mean they had to leave the state.

The stories these parents and potential parents shared are about neither choice nor tragedy, so they did not fit in any of the reductive models our culture offers. While the stories challenge our cultural stereotypes and misunderstandings of Down syndrome, they also pose a more broad-based challenge to conventional feminist understanding of reproductive decision-making. Parents talked with me about how their experiences exceeded standard cultural frameworks. Several mothers supported the right to abortion but did not terminate their own pregnancies. They grappled with the vocabulary of *fetus* and *child*, a distinction that they found unclear and shifting. They addressed how the pregnant woman was the decision-maker, a situation they experienced as isolating rather than empowering. Ultimately, the interviews highlighted the inadequacy of the narrative of choice. Whereas many feminists tend to equate choice with the right to have an abortion, many women in my interviews chose to keep their pregnancies in the face of pressure to terminate. Whereas feminists often present choice as an enabling necessity, my interview subjects experienced it as a wrenching burden. Whereas feminism elevates and empowers the individual, these stories show such positioning to be painful and isolating. Ultimately, my interviews reveal choice to be an inadequate framework for understanding what these women thought they were doing.

Many women describe wrestling with the kind of fears and negative messages about disability expressed by the feminist narratives described in the previous section. When Wolf writes that she "respected and admired women who could give their lives over to caring for a severely disabled child, but I knew I could not do it myself," she reiterates the myth of the saintly mother, in which women who parent children with disabilities are figured as exceptionally virtuous, strong, and self-sacrificing. However, many of my subjects felt just as undone by a fetal diagnosis as Wolf or Richards imagine they would be. Amy said that when she learned her child had Down syndrome, "I wailed. I don't know if you can imagine the most gut-wrenching wail a grown woman can make, but it is a sound I will never forget, and hope no woman ever has to utter. But that sound came out of my throat!" A couple of interview subjects shared the view, reinforced in feminist writings, that the fetus is defective, worthless, or tragic. Kilolo told me, "I was completely devastated. I felt like the rug had been pulled out from under me. The 'why me' questions. I was very tearful. I remember I cried and I—I wanted a drink. I remember saying to myself, 'Well, what difference would it make anyway?' You know, they say alcohol could potentially damage your fetus, and it's already done." Kathryn recalled leaving the appointment where an ultrasound strongly suggested the fetus had Down syndrome:

KATHRYN: I drove home, and there's a waste management company in our area named Grace. It was trash day, so I saw rows of trash cans, because this company had given everybody trashcans with their logo. I was riding down the street seeing Grace, Grace, Grace. I knew our daughter's name was going to be Grace, and I was like, "Really, a trash can? Fuck no."

ALISON: Did it feel like a repeated message, like some bad movie where the name keeps popping up?

KATHRYN: Yes. It was like a cheesy Hallmark movie. And then I had this picture in my head. She was standing there in the sun, and it was like, it's okay, *that's* my girl.

We were both on lunch breaks when we had this conversation. I was in my empty office in Charleston, and she was in hers in Saint Louis. I listened to her voice, to her pauses as she teared up and waited to calm down enough that she'd be able to explain. She told me, "I was not raised in a church. I don't think I believe in God—I can't even decide if *god* should be capitalized." But she felt that this trash can message was "kind of meant to be."

Her God-inflected, nonreligious experience has emerged in large part from her life with her daughter, as she explains on her blog:

It is a fucking miracle we are here, and if we are lucky enough to make it then we should take full advantage of the world God has given us. I am newly and acutely aware that taking advantage doesn't necessarily mean college, travel, and catching the latest gallery opening. Sometimes it just means blowing bubbles in the grass and throwing the dog's Kong. There's a lot of crap online about being "chosen" and "special kids for special parents." I am loath to join that crowd—they seem to be the same people who believe God supports their football team and doesn't notice the starving babies because their particular denomination doesn't have a building in that particular country. I am much more comfortable being a statistical freak. But though I may not believe in God, I believe he passed over my neighbors and gave me my daughter, and I am profoundly and deeply grateful He did.

When I read this story online, I started crying. I later told Kathryn, "This is the *me* moment, too. I don't have any religious beliefs, and I would have thought Maybelle was a terrible burden, but instead she's a fabulous gift."

Kathryn's story reveals a number of things. She searches for the words and images to help her explain an experience that doesn't fit within the available narratives. She swears and discusses God, describing her experience as "a fucking miracle." Although she laughs at the notion that she received a universal message from trash cans, the moment of seeing her daughter's name again and again was both funny and significant. It was "a cheesy Hallmark movie," and yet it was also a moment where—driving home pregnant—she saw her daughter standing in the sun and thought, "That's my girl." She offers a story that's filled with contradictions. She doesn't believe in God, but she believes her daughter is a gift from that God.

Her daughter has expanded her world in ways she finds difficult to describe. Kathryn's experience resonates with many of the stories I heard in my research, and with my own experience. Before Maybelle's birth, I would have suspected that the "right" use of prenatal technology would be to terminate the pregnancy if I had learned that the fetus had a disability. I would have thought this largely because I understood Down syndrome to be something tragic and frightening. Like a commenter on my *Motherlode* article, I thought that "a condition that brings with it guaranteed cognitive disabilities is not something I'm willing to inflict on another human being, much less my own beloved child." Because I'm a college professor, I value intellect. I care far less about my appearance, current trends, or the amount of money I earn than I do about intelligence. The ability to analyze the world, to pose questions and gather evidence, and to communicate findings has been central to my identity. I would have thought it would be awful to have a person with an intellectual disability in my family.

And yet as my life with Maybelle shows me, intellect doesn't define human validity. It was surprisingly easy for me to let go of my expectation that she would attend the prestigious academic magnet school, because I quickly began recognizing that a fully human life takes many forms, as do the joy and connection that help create family and community. As Kathryn said, sometimes a valuable life "just means blowing bubbles in the grass and throwing the dog's Kong." I'm having a very happy life with my daughter. My values have broadened. What I value for myself can be different from what I value for Maybelle, and I've begun to recognize that I no longer want Maybelle to be a miniature version of me.

Although mothering Grace isn't what Kathryn would have predicted—or requested—she is "deeply grateful" and committed to making the world a better place for Grace. Indeed, Grace seems like a significant choice for her daughter's name, since *grace* is an unexpected, uncontrolled gift. Three of the mothers I talked with named their daughters Grace. I offer this observation not as a religious message but as a way of thinking about how to change the game.

For Meriah, the decision to keep her pregnancy led to endless agonizing. "My angst over our decision to keep her consumed me, kept me awake for most of my pregnancy, endless insomnia. Night after night I'd relive my own most horrific memories, wondering if I made the right choice, if I had simply conscripted my daughter to a life of misery." Steven, the father of a child with Down syndrome, recalls that his own mother found the news of a prenatal diagnosis "absolutely devastating" and "an absolute funeral."

According to a familiar explanatory narrative, people who don't terminate pregnancies when fetal disability is identified are motivated by ideological or religious reasons.[23] My interviews challenge that explanation, revealing a far more diverse array of reasoning. Some of the women I interviewed chose not to have testing because of their religious beliefs. They believed that testing for anomalies is appropriate only when you might choose to terminate; because they had religious objections to termination, they did no screening. One woman I interviewed identified very strongly as religious but opted to have an initial screening. When the results revealed that she had a higher-than-average possibility of having a child with Down syndrome, she decided to do no more testing. Other women made the same decisions without religious foundations.

Many characterized themselves as pro-choice, but their accounts demonstrate that the concept of choice is far too limited to explain their experiences. Tricia expressed a sentiment I heard repeatedly: "I'm pro-choice, but it's awfully complex when it's close to home."[24] At least three women I interviewed had had abortions in the past but did not terminate pregnancies with fetuses identified as having Down syndrome. Elizabeth was an activist for women's rights in many areas, including abortion. But she said she felt devastated by the decision to have an abortion in college: "After that time, I knew I would never have another abortion if I became pregnant unplanned. I would find a way to manage whatever the situation." She discussed a later pregnancy:

> With Rachel . . . she was so wanted by me. I planned her and did everything I could to get pregnant short of begging Dan for another child. The heart defect and then the Down syndrome were overwhelming pieces of news, and sometimes during the pregnancy I wondered if the baby might die before birth and all would be better for her. I attached these feelings to the heart defect (not Down syndrome) because we were unsure of the severity and how she would manage once born. I was so scared she would die shortly after birth. Never once considered terminating after we got the Down syndrome news.

Elizabeth's story reveals her mixed feelings: she thought that the pre-natal death of the fetus "would be better for her," but then she was "so scared [the baby] would die shortly after birth." She was certain that she wouldn't terminate the pregnancy, but she wasn't certain what would be best for the child.

Others grappled with the possibility of abortion more directly. Le-anne had had two abortions earlier in her life, when she wasn't ready to be a parent. When she was pregnant with her second child, amniocente-sis revealed that this fetus had Down syndrome.

> LEANNE: I was just kind of shell-shocked. I really actually went through the process of deciding whether or not to go through with [an abortion] or not. I had another ultrasound, and I was almost sure I couldn't do it. That I couldn't go down the path of terminat-ing. So, I would set up little things for myself. I would have an ul-trasound where they're really going to look at the heart. If anything was wrong, I wasn't going to go through with [the pregnancy], because it wasn't worth it for the child. When really, they could have surgery, you know. So, I said that that will make my decision, because I didn't really want to make that decision myself. I wanted something to determine it for me. If the heart's okay . . . then the heart was okay.
>
> ALISON: Was that a relief, or like, "Damn it, decision still not made"?
>
> LEANNE: Yeah, it was kind of like that.

For Leanne, the diagnosis of Down syndrome and the decision of whether to continue with the pregnancy were traumatic. She wasn't opposed to abortion in general terms, and she didn't perceive her earlier abortions as devastating, as Elizabeth had. For this preg-nancy, however, there was no easy decision and certainly none that fit with the familiar and limited range of available narratives about parenting.

As Leanne's story shows, the notion of choice, as it has been used in feminist defenses of reproductive freedom, doesn't effectively describe the experiences of pregnant women confronted with an unwelcome diagnosis. Leanne did not feel empowered by being the one who had to decide what to do. "I didn't really want to make that decision myself," she said, so she looked for reasons to terminate: "If anything was wrong, I wasn't going to go through with it." She was searching for a way out of "choice"—for validation or for some kind of assistance.

Another woman I interviewed also resisted the framework of individual choice. Diane became pregnant unexpectedly. She and her partner weren't sure that they wanted to continue with the pregnancy even before the testing began. In the wake of a prenatal diagnosis, Diane wanted external guidance. As she progressed in her pregnancy, she discovered that she kept moving the line to determine whether she would have an abortion: "I was already kind of in a situation where we were trying to decide—because it was such an unplanned thing and my boyfriend and I weren't together very long—whether he and I were even going to keep the baby regardless of what the testing told us. So we're still kind of, 'Do we even want to have the baby at all, regardless of whether it's Down syndrome, special needs, or whatever?'"

The prenatal testing became a way for her to try to gather information to decide whether to have an abortion. But she found it harder than expected to anticipate what she would do with the information she received. She initially thought that if the fetus had a disability, she'd terminate. When Down syndrome was identified, she changed her mind, telling herself that if the fetus had anything else, she'd terminate. Then when a significant heart condition was diagnosed, she decided that as long as the child could have a meaningful life, she would continue, but if the child's life was in danger, she'd terminate. When testing revealed that the child's life was in danger, she discovered that she still wasn't ready to terminate. "We got to the point of the amnio," she said. "We had already named him, I had already seen him a couple of times, and you know, he was my son. And regardless of whatever issues he had, he was still my child, and I was going to go through with it. And if that meant, you know, a long, hard road for me, then that's what it was going to have to be. But I still got thinking in my head, just Down syndrome. When we get to something else, that's like hitting another brick wall and I had to start all over again."

While feminists insist, for ideological reasons, on the term *fetus*, Diane, who had formerly felt fairly certain she would have an abortion, reported knowing that this was her son, her child, a person who already had a name. She felt ready for whatever challenges his life might pose for her. She didn't frame her experience using an easy binary of tragedy versus bliss; instead, she identified parenthood as "a long, hard road." And yet even after regarding the fetus as a person, Diane was still uncertain whether she would or should continue the pregnancy. It was never intuitively obvious to her, since each new diagnosis required her to "start all over again." Diane explained how the heart diagnosis affected her decision: "His heart defect made things more complicated, more and more complicated—as if it could get any more complicated." But it did get more complicated. After the amniocentesis identified the fetus as having Down syndrome and a cardiology visit identified a very serious heart defect (the cardiologist characterized the fetus as having a 20 percent chance of survival), she and her boyfriend had different opinions—he wanted to terminate, she wanted to have "her baby." So, she said, they "compromised": she would carry the pregnancy to term, but then they wouldn't do surgery. They would wait and let the baby die. Her son did not die and, at the time of our interview, was eighteen months old and healthy.

In our conversation, Diane revealed the complexity of her thinking in the absence of available narrative frameworks for explaining her experience. A feminist assertion of Diane's right to choose doesn't help her figure out what *choice* means under her individual circumstances. She knew that she had a choice, but she wanted something more: guidance, information, real options, meaningful support.

Advocates of abortion rights often focus on the importance of individual autonomy in reproductive decision-making. They seek to empower pregnant women by giving them control over their own bodies. This right to decide is, of course, legally appropriate. But we have seen how the women I interviewed felt more burdened than empowered by having to bear responsibility for their decisions. Several women said that they disagreed with their partners about whether to have an abortion. While Diane was still trying to decide what to do, her partner was scheduling an abortion. Diane explained, "I think that's really where he thought we were going to go, and I wasn't saying no at that point. I was just saying, 'I don't know, I don't know, I don't know.'" Many of the women with whom I spoke understood themselves to have a clear difference of opinion from their male partners. Julia, who was pregnant at the time of our interview, had an older child with Down syndrome and had just recently had an amniocentesis for this second pregnancy. She was anticipating disagreement with her husband about what to do if the results showed that the fetus had Down syndrome.

> ALISON: So, did this really feel to you like your decision?
> JULIA: Yes, which made it so much harder because I knew he would never do it.
> ALISON: He would never terminate the pregnancy?
> JULIA: No.

Pregnant women can feel pressure from partners and family members who disagree with their decisions. Reproductive rights activism typically concentrates on giving women access to abortion. However, many women I interviewed expressed surprise at the extent to which they felt an openness to termination from people who they had understood to be explicitly opposed to abortion. For instance, Leanne's parents said they would support her whatever she decided, and she seemed to feel this as a slap in the face.

> LEANNE: I thought, excuse me? I just didn't expect that from my parents. My mother's a solid Christian, and my dad's a retired pastor.
>
> ALISON: So you felt like they were saying that if you decide to terminate, that it's okay?
>
> LEANNE: Yeah. Maybe even more for my mother.

Although Leanne's parents said that the decision was all hers, she felt that they were giving her the message that she should terminate, thus adding to her feeling of isolation as she contemplated keeping the pregnancy. At this moment, she was eager for a different kind of support, a family community that would help her navigate having a child with a disability.

An emphasis on individual choice permeates much writing about reproductive rights, but these interviews demonstrate that individual rights and responsibilities don't solve all problems or even explain them. These women didn't discuss individualized decision-making as empowering, with meaningful options available to them. Instead, they felt frightened and pressured, as if those around them had unpredictable agendas that had to be negotiated and manipulated. Their stories relate complex experiences that need to appear in feminist discussions of reproduction. Women who support reproductive rights, even those who have had abortions, may still decide to have a child with Down syndrome. These narratives suggest that the idea of choice does not lead to easy or universal answers. Instead, reproductive decision-making is messy and sometimes painful. It often involves negotiations beyond those connoted by the term *choice*. Moreover, in reproductive rights rhetoric, *choice* generally refers to the availability of abortion, but this wasn't the focus for the parents and potential parents in my sample. Reproductive decisions may rest on an individual woman, but they require support from family, community, and medical services. Certainly the people I interviewed challenge our cultural stereotypes and misunderstandings of Down syndrome, but they also challenge our feminist understanding of reproductive rights. A better alternative is the more communal, social-justice-oriented discourse of reproductive justice.

Reproductive Justice

The scholarly and activist framework of reproductive justice expands conversations around a host of questions relating to reproduction. Rather than framing the central issue as choice, which, as we have seen, can focus unproductively on the individual woman, reproductive justice demands that we recognize social context, acknowledging how community opens and closes particular possibilities around reproduction. As Jael Silliman and her co-authors explain, it attends to "a much wider set of concerns. Access to resources and services, economic rights, freedom from violence, and safe and healthy communities are all integral to [this] expanded vision."[25] Reproductive justice also examines how stereotypes about race, class, and ability are created and perpetuated within narratives about reproductive decision-making. Alison Kafer notes how the rhetoric of choice may stigmatize women of color and poor women as bad decision-makers and reinforce ableist notions about which choices are valid and deserving of social support.[26] The concept of reproductive justice acknowledges the complexity I have found lacking in the more familiar feminist conversations about reproductive rights.

Reproductive rights discourse generally adopts an individualized framework in addressing abortion law. Of course, an individual woman needs to decide about her own reproduction.[27] But this model has its limits. My interviews reveal that parents and potential parents may object to this individualized expectation. They recognize that decision-making happens in an intimate and a societal context. They want a *we* framework, not an *I* framework, and they resist the simplistic notion of choice because they recognize that they are being asked to do something far more interdependent than this atomized term suggests.

Reproductive justice asks scholars to view reproduction as something that extends far beyond the individual. Legal scholar Dorothy Roberts makes this point clearly: "Reproductive liberty must encompass more than the protection of an individual woman's choice to end her pregnancy. It must encompass the full range of procreative activities, including the ability to bear a child, and it must acknowledge that we make reproductive decisions within a social context, including inequalities of wealth and power. Reproductive freedom is a matter of social justice, not individual choice."[28]

According to Roberts, the focus on individual women's access to abortion is narrow and misguided, absent a broader approach to the context in which such decisions are embedded. Similarly, Katz Rothman criticizes a social system that "fails to take collective responsibility for the needs of its members, and leaves individual women to make impossible choices. We are spared collective responsibility, because we individualize the problem. We make it the woman's own. She 'chooses,' and so we owe her nothing. Whatever the cost, she has chosen, and now it is her problem, not ours."[29] Both scholars, like many others in this vein, identify reproductive decision-making as extending beyond individual choice, and they stress the importance of the community.[30] Observing how the emphasis on choice places women of color, women who are poor, and people with disabilities at a disadvantage, Kafer notes that reproductive justice offers the tools for a "cross-movement analysis" to bring together reproduction and disability.[31]

My conversations demonstrated again and again the inadequacy of *choice* as a label for women's experiences. The people I spoke with felt pressed to make individual choices even as they were aware of operating "within a social context," as Roberts acknowledges. This social context is multilayered, from the intimate to the institutional, and includes inequalities of class, race, ability, and authority. It plays a large role in dictating the value of the fetus and framing certain choices as more reasonable or ethical than others. It generates stereotypes that influence not only individual beliefs but also the support systems available to children and families. Most of the individuals I talked with brought up the impact of such social factors on their decision-making.

The role of kinship and social networks in which parents and potential parents are operating came up in every interview I conducted. Parents and potential parents, particularly those who anticipate that relatives would play a large part in their child's life, care a great deal about the responses of their families. Often, the families expressed a range of opinions. The interviewees also discussed responses from their friends, coworkers, and other people they encounter daily.

My conversation with Aasha, a single mother, gives a clear example of how these community circumstances can affect decision-making. She described how she negotiated within family, friends, and broader social environments. Aasha described herself as having initially believed the stereotyped, negative perspectives about having a child with a disability. After the amniocentesis let her know her fetus had Down syndrome, she saw herself facing "the end of the world." Her understanding of what parenting a child with Down syndrome would mean was shaped by societal distortions and misunderstandings. She gathered her entire family together to tell them the news because she wanted them to help her make a decision. She reported that her mother said, "Have an abortion," while most others felt that she should "bear her cross," meaning that she should remain pregnant, but with an awareness of her tragic circumstances. Then she recalled a pivotal moment: "One of the turning points in that family meeting was my stepmother. . . . She just started crying in the meeting, and she could barely get it out, but she said to the group, 'Just have the baby and I will raise her.'"

The emotional reaction of Aasha's stepmother was significant: she humanized the child by offering to raise her, framing her not as a cross to bear but as a person with a valuable life. Aasha continued: "Her statement to me and the family was one of the deciding factors for me to take abortion off the table." It didn't matter why her stepmother said what she said; it only mattered that she said it. By describing the outcome of the pregnancy as a "baby" and voicing her desire for it to live, the stepmother activated a possibility that changed Aasha's thinking. Aasha explained how important it was that she gain the explicit support of her family: "I also knew that I had everybody's [support]—at least their verbal commitment to this process—because I told them all, I said (you know, at the time I was finishing my doctorate degree and I was working full-time and my family didn't live in the immediate area), . . . I just needed them to know I will need all of [their] support to make this happen. And they gave me their word, their commitment. So I—it brought me comfort." The demonstrations of family support helped make Aasha's decision possible.

At the same time that she was having this conversation with her family, Aasha's engagement with a broader community also helped with her decision-making. Her culture had provided her with various negative attitudes about having a child with Down syndrome, and most of the people she encountered endorsed those opinions by offering comfort in the face of what they understood to be a tragedy. However, one person offered a different view. Shortly after her amniocentesis, Aasha met with a friend who was a social worker. Aasha recalled the encounter: "And I told her that, you know, my baby's going to have Down syndrome. And we're riding up the elevator and she was just quiet. Then, all of a sudden . . . she starts rattling off resources. And I said to her, 'Did you hear what I just said? I just said, you know, it's the end of the world. I just said I'm going to have a baby with Down syndrome, and you're already talking about resources.'" Notably, her friend disagreed, viewing Aasha's situation not as a tragedy but as one requiring support and resources:

And she was like, "Well, I'm a social worker so my thing is if you've got a 'problem,' let's start talking about how we can address the problem. . . . You know, what supports do you need?" Like, she just went on this whole thing about how can I get support in all kinds of forms. You know, monetary, social support, physical, medical support, all of that. She just looked at it from a different perspective than I did, and she came at it different than anyone else had. And that was also a turning point for me, that why does she not see it so negatively? . . . It was something I will always remember because she was the first person who didn't say, you know, something like "Oh, Aasha, that's terrible," or "Oh, I feel so bad for you." She didn't say that at all. It was, "Okay, well, we've got some work to do." You know, so she really helped me kind of reframe my situation where it wasn't total doom and gloom.

Aasha's friend framed the child not as a terrible misfortune but as a person for whom varieties of support could be gathered. Her perspective helped undo what disability studies scholar Adrienne Asch identifies as the "sin of synecdoche." That sin, Asch explains, "is to allow a single known characteristic of the future child to so overwhelm and negate all other hoped-for attributes that the prospective parents no longer desire the coming-into-being of that child."[32] Aasha's friend did not let Down syndrome become the only significant characteristic of the child. She recognized that Aasha was not an isolated individual but a member of a community, and the friend identified levels of support ("monetary, social support, physical, medical") that the new mother and her child would need to thrive.

Aasha said that after she decided that she was going to have her daughter, her pregnancy was "wonderful." She described a baby shower that included eighty people: "It really was a celebration in my mind of people committed to support, you know, in their own individual way—but it was just this sense of community rallying around not me, but this baby."

ALISON: So you really did, then, feel like you had—you had a community. Like she was being born into a place where people were excited about her and were going to love her and support her.

AASHA: Yeah. Absolutely. And, like, I felt like I could just relax and just—literally just deliver her. I felt very comfortable. Because I think for me it was just about the loneliness of it all. Like I just knew I couldn't do this by myself. You know. And maybe I said it enough times to where people said, "Okay. Okay. We will help you."

Aasha's story demonstrates the importance of community as a component of reproductive decision-making, and the layers of social context that are involved. Notably, Aasha framed these conversations with different members of her community as turning points. She didn't make her decision alone, even though, as a single mother, she might be operating in a more individualized situation than that of expectant parents who are partnered. Her decision was complex and grounded in a communal *we*.

Aasha's story makes an important point that extends beyond her own pregnancy and the knowledge that her fetus had a genetic disability. Her experience is applicable for broader feminist conversations about reproduction. No parent is actually an *I*—we are always a *we* since parenting a child always requires a community. Kimala Price explains that the reproductive justice movement's "three core values" are "the right to have an abortion, the right to have children, and the right to parent those children."[33] Price argues that if we want women to have control over their reproduction, this power means more than the ability to choose not to be pregnant. It also means that they can choose to have children and to parent them effectively, an aspect of reproductive rights that many feminist scholars have overlooked.

This observation was certainly meaningful to the parents I interviewed. Perhaps even more pointedly, the former social justice organization Generations Ahead echoes several reproductive justice advocates from the Global South in calling for "a framing away from the right not to have children to a right to have children, and a framing away from creating a self-sufficient, productive individual to re-shaping society to provide for the needs of all people, regardless of gender, race, ability, sexual orientation, citizenship status and class."[34] The need for community support may be more visible when a person is parenting a child with a disability, but dependence is part of the human condition, as Garland-Thomson notes.[35] A continued emphasis on the individual can perpetuate what Aasha described as "the loneliness of it all." Parenting is never something a person can do entirely alone.

As socially conservative state governments pass laws making abortion less attainable by cutting funds to Planned Parenthood, requiring lengthier waiting periods or transvaginal ultrasounds, feminists might be tempted to double down on the defense of individual women's access to safe and legal abortion. But a truly just conversation about reproduction requires that feminist scholars respond to and respect the complexity of women's decisions. We not only need to respect the humanity of people with disabilities but also need to help create communities that make decisions possible. The concept of reproductive justice provides an alternative model that would "emphasize the relationship of reproductive rights to human rights and economic justice."[36] Emphasizing social justice, the model recognizes that reproductive decisions take place within a broader set of community priorities.

Reproductive justice provides a framework for a world in which individual women are part of broader social networks and in which decision-making is informed by complex interactions among individuals, families, and society. Whereas reproductive choice narrowly focuses on an individual selecting the most appropriate of her options, reproductive justice recognizes that sometimes there is no good option. A longtime *Star Trek* fan, I'm reminded of the story of the Kobayashi Maru, a no-win game used to test the discipline and character of cadets at the Starfleet Academy. Captain James T. Kirk is the only person ever to have "won"—because he undermined the game. He recognized that it was rigged: everyone was supposed to lose, and yet they were forced to play anyway. So he cheated. The analogue for cheating in the context of disability and reproductive decision-making is refusing to accept the either-or options seemingly represented by the notion of choice. Like Captain Kirk, many of the parents I interviewed recognized they were being asked to play a game that is desperate and unfair. They recognized that they might be bringing a person they already love into a hostile world. Instead of accepting that dilemma, they decided that they would change the world. As one father explained, "The hardest part about being a parent isn't her diagnosis or medical condition or cognitive delays or what have you. It's really about dealing with acceptance in society." This father has made it part of his life's work to advocate for acceptance. He has become an activist. And, like Captain Kirk, he is changing the game.

3

The Welcome Table

Since Maybelle was eighteen months old, she's been able to sign and sing along with a song called "The Welcome Table." It's an old gospel song on one of her children's CDs, with voices that break from unison into beautiful, mournful, and hopeful harmonies:

> I'm gonna sit at the welcome table.
> I'm gonna sit at the welcome table one of these days,
> Hallelujah!
> I'm gonna sit at the welcome table,
> Sit at the welcome table one of these days. One of these days.

The song ends with an acapella verse, with the harmonies floating out there:

> All God's children gonna sit together.
> All God's children gonna sit together one of these days,
> Hallelujah!
> All God's children gonna sit together.
> All God's children gonna sit together one of these days.
> One of these days.

When Maybelle first learned the song, she wanted to hear it repeatedly. We'd be sitting together at the dining room table, and she'd demand, "Again!" when the song finished.

I wanted to hear it too. I'd listen, watching Maybelle's face, her smiles. I'd watch her accurately sign the song with her fat fingers and dimpled knuckles. Even now, years later, when I hear the song, I still find my hands clasping for the sign "together"—a circle coming out from my heart and returning. Even now, I can get teary listening to it, feel the softening in my chest. *Together* is a word that makes me cry, that makes me feel gratitude for having this child in my life. Gratitude that we get to experiment with what it means to be a family. That we get to experience moving through the world together. And the space to frame this connection is the table: where we eat together.

Over the years, I noticed that the metaphor of the table kept coming up in conversations about disability. Talking with parents, reading the words of parents and advocates, I heard echoes of Maybelle's favorite gospel song. "We have to share the table." "Who's at the table?" "We've got to sit at the table." "I sat at the table and noticed how exclusive it was." At first, I assumed that the repetition of this phrase was a coincidence—a familiar turn of phrase that isn't grounded in actually sitting together. But it came up often enough that I knew I had to pay attention.

As I was considering the meaning of eating together, I thought of the late disability rights activist Harriet McBryde Johnson. She identified ways that the world can exclude and dehumanize—"a world that by and large thinks it would be better if people like me did not exist." She went on to explain: "My fight has been for accommodation, the world to me, and me to the world," and she presents sharing a meal as a way to encourage accommodation.[1]

In her memoir, *Too Late to Die Young*, Johnson recounts a visit with Peter Singer, a philosopher who has argued—rationally but distressingly and persistently in his academic work—that the lives of people with disabilities like Johnson's are "worse off" and therefore they should be aborted, euthanized, or, as adults, given access to physician-assisted suicide. Johnson accepts Singer's invitation to Princeton University for a series of conversations with students in which she and he can offer opposing viewpoints. Although the visit is physically and cognitively challenging, Johnson perseveres.

Toward the end of her visit, Johnson joins Singer for a meal with some students. At one point, her elbow slips, and because of her degenerative neuromuscular disease, she's unable to feed herself. She needs an adjustment. She writes, "Normally I get whoever is on my right hand to do this sort of thing. Why not now? I gesture to Singer. He leans over and I whisper. 'Grasp this wrist and pull forward one inch, without lifting.' He looks a little surprised but follows my instructions to the letter."[2] This incident is crucial to her impression of Singer. Although Singer is often criticized—accurately, I think—as being an advocate for genocide, Johnson recounts this moment in her book with a kind of wry tenderness. The anecdote is not merely ironic; instead, it suggests that despite his academic arguments, Singer's experience eating with Johnson humanized them both. Johnson wasn't an abstract concept but was a woman who needed his help to continue their meal together. For her part, Johnson writes, "And then, the hard part: I've come to believe that Singer actually is human, even kind in his way."[3] This shift happened to her in part because of her experimentation. "Why not now?" she asks. And that interaction allows her to experience a complex, messy set of responses to Singer.

In his eulogy about Johnson for the *New York Times*, Singer reminisces with a similar tenderness about assisting Johnson during their shared dinner. He writes that Johnson's description of their meal "suggests that she saw me not simply as 'the enemy' but as a person with whom it was possible to have some forms of human interaction." And he identifies her as a person whose "life was evidently a good one."[4] By allowing herself to be vulnerable at the table, Johnson gave Singer the opportunity to recognize that although she depended on others for help, she was nonetheless a person, not an abstract concept to be wished away. Eating together—that physical act—was crucial, and it led to meaningful connection.

* * *

This account doesn't mean that the physical act of eating is some sort of rainbow of transformation. Down syndrome, like many other disabilities, can present eating challenges. It can be frustrating as hell. Several of the women I talked with described their vulnerabilities. Kilolo wrote emphatically, "When my daughter [Jade] was a baby, she had to be on special formula (Nutramigen/$27 per can!!!!). It was something my other mommy-friends didn't have to deal with. My daughter was also fed through a feeding tube (NG [nasogastric] and NJ [nasojejunal] tubes) for a long while."

Tricia also wrote me about the suffering she endured around meals with Georgia. When Georgia was an infant, "her issue was that she was born with four holes in her heart and she could not sustain the suck motion for long enough to get adequate nutrition. . . . It was not the best of times. We went to a week long in-hospital nutrition clinic because she had failure to thrive." Tricia described later meals with an older Georgia as a nightmare: "At some point [Georgia] began throwing her plate/bowl at EVERY SINGLE MEAL. Dinnertime felt AWFUL. It was such a struggle and it felt futile." She described it as "a HUGE source of anxiety for me." She continued: "All the struggle around food made it feel like the worst time(s) of our day. I DREADED dinner. I always wanted to sit down and eat as a family, but Alex and I would wait to eat until after [the kids] went to bed: 1. less gross, and 2. We were eating different things because the kids were so picky."

And yet, because of Tricia and Alex's consistent, dedicated, and difficult work, meals improved: "Things are much better. When we all sit down to eat, it's actually enjoyable. In fact, I am still a bit in shock every time." Georgia no longer throws bowls. The family can be together, even to eat together. (The painful, exhausting, and challenging mealtimes Tricia endured with Georgia don't strike me as significantly different from what my friends with typical kids tell me about their own experiences.)

Eating with a disabled child can also be a barrier to connection with a larger community. Tricia sounded alone when she described struggling with her daughter's "failure to thrive." Kilolo told me about being distanced from her "mommy-friends" and being limited at the "tables" where she sat with others.

What Kilolo described to me doesn't seem to be about a medical condition. Instead, it's about loneliness. Tricia, too, emailed me, attempting to help me understand being in a hospital, being a mother who's struggling with her daughter's failure to thrive—and it's not about the support she and her husband got from their community. It's entirely possible that Tricia and Kilolo received a great deal of support from their friends and families, but when they shared these memories with me, both women sounded isolated.

When I emailed Kilolo for a follow-up conversation, she talked with me about what it means to eat together. In particular, she wrote about her daughter's experiences at the age of eight: "My daughter gets invited to kid birthday parties frequently, but as I reflect, they're the parties of close family and friends. My daughter hasn't been invited to the birthday parties, events, or activities of her schoolmates." Her email described a significant shift in her understanding of Jade's inclusion. She started out describing her daughter as a child included in the community, but in explaining this to me, she began identifying ways her daughter was excluded. Her daughter wasn't part of her schoolmates' parties; she was not welcome. Kilolo immediately identified this situation as a problem that she, as Jade's mother, had created: "The 'tables' she and I join are where I feel most comfortable. I haven't done much reaching out beyond my small tables."

And yet this situation doesn't strike me as a problem that Kilolo or Jade caused. Instead, it was a problem created by how her daughter's schoolmates viewed her—and this exclusion results from larger societal stigma. Jade's time in her school system was somewhat segregated: she had many of her classes with other children with disabilities. Schoolmates like Jade's have been taught that she doesn't belong. They've been taught that the table is a place where she isn't recognized as "one of us."

At almost every level, then, eating is a way of assigning status. Both Kilolo and Tricia experience eating as a space that makes other things visible: it's not merely a literal challenge but also a struggle to connect. In other words, eating can function as both literal and metaphorical. Kilolo's story strikes me as a place where the metaphorical meets the lived experience. "At the table" isn't simply a metaphor.

* * *

I was already thinking about the meanings of the phrase *at the table* when I interviewed Nancy Brown and her twenty-five-year-old daughter Bridget, who has Down syndrome. When Nancy and I talked, I noticed that she often used the phrase *at the table* to illustrate what it means when current organizations—even Down syndrome advocacy groups—fail to include people with Down syndrome in their meetings, conferences, or advisory boards.

"I am continually surprised," she said, "as I work in different agencies and organizations throughout Illinois but also connect with national stuff." She immediately framed her observations in terms of understanding herself as an activist: "It starts with us. It starts with having people at the table who actually have Down syndrome. There's a bunch of people doing a lot of work about people with disabilities and not sitting at the table with them." She talked about Bridget's role in organizations, such as the Illinois State Board of Education, that could take part in making inclusion real at a larger level: "If [Bridget] can't come with me, I'm not going. If she can't sit at the table—because I'm tired of seeing all these agencies and organizations, all these wonderful, you know, bleeding-heart people sitting around talking about how wonderful it is having a lovely lunch, while the person with the disability is sitting home eating potato chips in front of a TV."

Although Bridget had been invited to do a presentation for the Illinois Board of Education—a meaningful opportunity to share her opinions and lived experiences—she was not included in the lunch meeting.

Potato chips in front of the TV are delicious, of course, but when she was not invited to eat with the others, her absence at the lunch became a symbol of her exclusion.

Nancy had other examples. One of the most surprising of them involved a fundraiser for an organization that supports people with disabilities. The event featured a speech by Desmond Tutu. Inviting an activist who has spent his life working for human rights to support an organization that works for people like Bridget would seem to be an ideal occasion for people with and without disabilities to come together. Instead, Bridget was one of the only people with disabilities at the event. Nancy shared her astonishment: "What does he think? He's looking out here at all these people, and, you know, we're talking about people with disabilities." From Nancy's perspective, the event became centered on the fundraisers. She told me, "We can't just raise money for people with disabilities. We have to sit at the table with them. We have to. You know, we actually have to be part of people's lives."

For Bridget and Nancy, the shared meal matters because it implies that everyone at the table is recognized as fully human. Bridget and Nancy have a phrase that describes this: "We segregate those we don't value." They're right to see this exclusion from the table as a version of segregation, designating those who are uninvited as *less than*. I immediately went online and had the phrase "We segregate those we don't value" made into a bumper sticker for my car.

* * *

This Easter, Maybelle and I had dinner with several families in our neighborhood. Maybelle sat at the kids' table, where the other children quickly picked up on her differences. Vivi asked me about Maybelle's speech. "Excuse me! Excuse me!" she said. "I'm only four, and I talk a lot! Maybelle is five, and I can't understand her." I told her, "Maybelle is different than you are. She's learning to talk, but she can't talk as well as you do yet." Vivi shrugged and returned to dinner. To the kids, these differences weren't obstacles or reasons to exclude; they were just differences—and eating together helped make that an ordinary part of life. Even though she couldn't talk as well as they did, the kids laughed with her—not at her—and helped her pick up her spoon when she dropped it. This is an example of experimenting with accommodation: Maybelle needed support from the other children, but she could also participate. I also held her to certain expectations, like using her napkin, sitting in her chair, and saying "oops" when she dropped her spoon rather than screaming in frustration. Rest assured these efforts weren't a 100 percent success. There were some screams of frustration and quite a bit of food rolling off her chin. "Maybelle," I'd say, "wipe your mouth, please!"

All the parents at the adult table looked over at their kids and offered support or discipline when it was needed. I was happy to discover that Maybelle wasn't the "problem child" at this event. In fact, there was no "problem child"—there were just children. One kid had eaten too much sugar and couldn't calm down. His parents had to stand up again and again to talk with him. Another child came over to the adult table to report on what other kids were eating. Another needed to wear her butterfly princess outfit to dinner. The adults rolled their eyes and shrugged: this is parenting. Is it outstanding parenting? Who knows. But I felt surprised and relieved that the primary form of difference that evening was between the kids' table and the adults' table. It wasn't about Maybelle's having Down syndrome; she was just a kid eating dinner, along with the others.

* * *

While parents are working toward creating particular versions of family and community, adults with Down syndrome are working on their own versions. In my conversations with them, too, mealtime kept coming up. Sam, a twenty-four-year-old student at an inclusive college, told me a story about his high school cafeteria:

SAM: When I was in high school, I got some friends to eat with. And that's kind of cool for me. And I'd get in a little trouble with someone. And I thought, "Okay. This is not a good idea to do that."

ALISON: What was troublesome?

SAM: It was like I'd meet someone with a mouthful and I thought, "Ah. Not a good idea."

ALISON: Oh, like one of your friends at the table was kind of gross?

SAM: Yeah. And I thought, "Okay. I'm not doing that."

ALISON: And so you stopped sitting with them?

SAM: Yeah.

This isn't the story of a kid with Down syndrome being excluded; it's about the kid with Down syndrome doing what high school kids do, making a judgment call and finding another place to eat.

Bridget Brown's story of high school is something like Sam's. She has always lived in the same town, where her mother, Nancy, was a tireless advocate for full inclusion. Nancy created social and peer-mentor circles for Bridget, helping to develop groups of typical students who—from preschool on—saw Bridget as "one of us." These students could help Bridget with curricular challenges and social interactions. Bridget told me that in her book group, they read books and then watch the movies based on those books. I asked her if the groups were fun. She said, "It is fun. And easy." She paused and told me, "Junk food." I laughed and told her that food was also a crucial part of the book group I used to belong to. Only when our laps were full of cookies or spanakopita or peach cobbler would we delve into the book itself.

Then she told me about a different group that she belongs to and that plays the dice game Bunco: "So this couple that I know for a long time, they both decided to do Bunco. It's a group of people with disabilities in Naperville, and we get together with them. What we do is we roll dice for, like, one dice for one, then two, then three, and then four and five and six. The dice. And then, at the end, around eightish, we have pizza.

Sometimes we do tacos. Sometimes we do other different types of food." Meals were a defining component of Bridget's fun with her friends. She knew details about the game and equivalent details about the dinner they'd have after: pizza or tacos, or "other different types of food." Food didn't replace the book or the game, but it helped to bring the group together.

Emily Kingsley told me a similar story about Jason. She was talking about her son's life as an adult, living in a house with two roommates who also have intellectual disabilities. Her particular example of what Jason's life was like was a meal:

> Saturday night, he and his roommates send out to the neighborhood pizza place. They send out. They use their own money, and they send out. And they have Netflix, and they have a movie night. They decide what movie they want to watch. And they make popcorn. So that's their movie night at their house.
>
> And I keep encouraging them. I say, "You guys, go to the movies yourselves. You can do it. You can go to the movies. You can go out to a restaurant yourself." They say, "Well, we're happier staying at home. We're fine."

Emily has mixed feelings about the meal and the evening activities that Jason and his roommates have created. She tells me this story in part to demonstrate that "they're not very self-motivating." The story is part of her explanation of her sadness that Jason is not living the life she thought he'd live when she was doing such intense activism, trying to make his life "like everybody else's."

It can be hard to know how to interpret these stories. Are Bridget and Jason providing evidence of change that should happen but hasn't yet? Maybe. But that doesn't seem to be the whole story. Jason's pizza nights are also about defining himself as a person and creating his own standards along with his friends. Bridget's book group and Bunco group are spaces where she and her friends can connect, in part by eating things that they enjoy.

* * *

The ending verse of "The Welcome Table" is incredibly powerful to me because it recognizes a shared humanity. The phrase "All God's children" in the chorus is, of course, a description of a God whose love erases differences. The song says that this is the beauty of the welcome table. Even though I don't have a personal belief in God, I adore the song's vision of—even demand for—people with a variety of differences sharing the same table. This means differences as profound as those that Kate, Sam, Nancy, and Bridget have described. Differences as profound as those of all the people I've talked to. Liz's daughter Rosemary, climbing on the kitchen counter to procure a sweet potato. Tara's son Eon, wrestling playfully with his brothers. Candee's daughter Katie, living in a house with her boyfriend. Sam and Hope, attending college. Bridget, giving public lectures about how to create inclusion. And these differences are also as mundane as Maybelle's preschool expecting her to learn to behave, or Tricia and Alex working consistently to help Georgia not throw bowls across the room, or Barb's son Henry, spelling at grade level but not speaking. I'm not imagining a welcome table just for people with Down syndrome: it's also for other disabled adults, who don't have to be described as "normal" to be loved, valued, and included.

Michael Bérubé ends his book *Life as We Know It* with the table: "We used to say that we were setting a place for [his son Jamie] at our table, and we meant it as literally and as metaphorically as our language would allow." Michael lists many of the foods that Jamie has learned to enjoy. Then he says,

> Most of all, though, he's learned now to set a table. Although he folds the napkins badly and distributes the silverware somewhat randomly, he knows where to put the plates and where to get the forks, and he knows

how to set his own place, with his own plate, with his own fork and spoon that say "Jamie." My job, for now, is to represent my son, to set his place at our collective table. But I know I am merely trying my best to prepare for the day he sets his own place. For I have no sweeter dream than to imagine—aesthetically and ethically and parentally—that Jamie will some-day be his own advocate, his own author, his own best representative.[5]

I love this conclusion to Michael's book. The place at the table is where Michael expresses his love, where Jamie is beginning to learn the process and will ultimately set his own place. Of course, this paragraph *always* makes me cry.

Early in my career at the College of Charleston, and long before May-belle was born, Harriet McBryde Johnson sent me an email, alerting me to the fact that the Women's and Gender Studies Program I was di-recting was hosting an event whose venue was inaccessible to people using wheelchairs. I was a good enough feminist to recognize the need for basic accommodations. It was a first step to commit to spaces that were accessible: we'll have plenty of tables for everybody! Now, six years later, I'm moving beyond that initial understanding of accommodation. I want accommodation to mean that we are reimagining our commu-nities in significant ways, that we are conceiving of our world as made better—richer—more wonderful by the inclusion of all kinds of diver-sity, including the diversity of physical and intellectual disabilities. I want us to bring our whole selves to the table, one table that everyone has the chance to sit at, a table where we're all truly welcome.

4

Saints, Sages, and Victims

Down Syndrome and Parental Narrative

The world wants our lives to fit into a few rigid narrative templates: how I conquered disability (and others can conquer their Bad Things!), how I adjusted to disability (and a positive attitude can move mountains!), how disability made me wise (you can only marvel and hope it never happens to you!), how disability brought me to Jesus (but redemption is waiting for you if only you pray). For me, living a real life has meant resisting those formulaic narratives.
—Harriet McBryde Johnson, *Too Late to Die Young: Nearly True Tales from a Life*

Parenting a (disabled) child can be tiring, distressing, upsetting and heartbreaking. It can also be rewarding, affirming, enjoyable and heartwarming. We heard all of these emotions in the accounts of parents even during the shortest conversations.
—Janice McLaughlin, Dan Goodley, Emma Clavering, and Pamela Fisher, *Families Raising Disabled Children: Enabling Care and Social Justice*

A day after Maybelle was born, her diagnosis with Down syndrome was confirmed. My reactions were complicated. Although I was grieving, I was wary of dehumanizing stories and incredibly aware of others' projections about the meaning of her disability. When one of the doctors in the NICU told me she was sorry that Maybelle has Down syndrome, I immediately told her that I didn't want my daughter's life to be seen as a tragedy. I had a friend tell my colleagues about Maybelle's diagnosis so that they would be prepared to tell me nothing but "Congratulations! What a beautiful baby!" I was holding a person who looked at me, who snuggled against my shoulder, who smelled milky and delicious, whose little hand wrapped around my finger. In those early days, I very strongly suspected that she was fully human, and I started looking for other stories, stories that described the child I was raising, stories that validated her full humanity.

A few days later, a close friend gave me Jennifer Graf Groneberg's *Road Map to Holland: How I Found My Way through My Son's First Two Years with Down Syndrome* (2008). She intuitively sensed that I needed a narrative to validate my daughter's existence, her personhood. I began reading the book, eager for this mother's story. I knew almost nothing about Down syndrome beyond a range of familiar cultural stereotypes, and I wanted both accurate information and—more importantly—a perspective that would help contextualize my life with my new daughter. I wanted encouragement and a clear picture of the joys and love that I hoped would still be part of our lives—something parents of typical kids have almost endless access to.

With effort, I made it a third of the way through the book. The effort was necessary because page after page offered the extremely detailed story of a mother's grief. When I encountered yet another description of grief—Groneberg's statement "Every time I think of Avery's Down syndrome, I start to cry. And I can barely manage our lives as it is"—I closed the book and put it away.[1] I was living in that place myself at the time and didn't need to experience another mother's suffering as well. The book only made me feel that the central experience of having a child with a disability is grief; reading the book provided none of the sustenance I'd been looking for.

When I returned to the book months later and read it through, I discovered that in the middle of the book, Groneberg narrates a turning point in her grieving, countering it by describing the positive experiences of having a child with a disability. This book, then, illustrates both the problems in, and the possibilities for, the genre of memoirs by parents of children with disabilities.

Problematically, this genre can fortify cultural stereotypes that portray children with disabilities as damaging forces in their parents' lives, as when Groneberg describes her life in terms of "despair. I'm the woman with the retarded son. It's a hurt so deep I only look at it when I'm forced to."[2] At the same time, however, parental memoirs can convey radically different notions of disability—notions enabled by intimate relationships and love. They can represent the child as a person who enriches his or her family. Sometimes the same book can do both these things, such as when Groneberg notes near the book's conclusion, "You can't have a child, any child, and not be changed by the experience. I'm changed by Avery. And the thing is, I don't want to be changed back."[3]

Life writing by and about people with disabilities—a genre G. Thomas Couser calls "the some body memoir"—is an important recent phenomenon.[4] A significant subset of these memoirs are written by parents of a child with a disability—often, but not always, a cognitive disability. These are the memoirs with which I'm concerned. As a parent of a child with a cognitive disability, I've read memoirs by other parents, hoping for a story that would enthusiastically affirm the full humanity of my child, frame her disability as an embraceable aspect of human diversity, and show me that my despair was emerging from misconception, not from the inherent defectiveness of my child. My hopes were often dramatically disappointed—but on occasion satisfied, too.

These memoirs are widely read, and not just by parents of children with disabilities; many are published by large mainstream presses and receive glowing reviews.[5] But parent memoir has received limited scholarly attention, including that from scholars in disability studies or those who focus on life writing.[6] I don't propose to offer a thorough survey of the genre as a whole; instead, I'm basing my observations about how the genre functions on a representative group of texts. These books reveal the powerful hold that formulaic narratives have, but they also offer glimpses of ways they can and should be resisted and overturned. They demonstrate that the family can both bolster oppressive cultural models of disability and profoundly challenge them.[7]

The Genre

G. Thomas Couser, the foremost scholar of disability memoir, notes that such narratives have an activist tendency: "What links these books is the fundamental endeavor to destigmatize various anomalous bodily conditions. Disability memoir should be seen, therefore, not as spontaneous self-expression but as a response—indeed a retort—to the traditional misrepresentation of disability in Western culture generally."[8] Similarly, Susannah Mintz notes that "autobiography might reinvent disability, for readers as much as writers, in dramatically liberatory ways."[9] But this potential isn't realized in most parent memoirs, and despite Couser's optimism about these memoirs, he, too, expresses concern about the political effects of a parental memoir. He asks how a person would feel reading a book that "describes people like you as not quite human and that is devoted explicitly to preventing the future (re)production of people like yourself?"[10]

While parental memoirs *can* serve activist or advocate roles, the genre is far more complicated than I expected.[11] Many of the parental memoirs I read reinforce our culture's dehumanizing stereotypes about disability. Through their use of grief and their emphasis on a limited medical model to depict the child's disabilities, these books often represent the child not as a person but as a problem for their parents to overcome.

In the first epigraph to this chapter, Harriet McBryde Johnson mentions the "formulaic narratives" that people with disabilities confront. She notes that for able-bodied people, disability often functions as a metaphor, an impetus for gratitude or religious commitment, or a sentimental lesson that warms the heart. While you might expect that parents of children with disabilities would see beyond cultural stereotypes to a complex lived reality, the truth is more complicated: although virtually all the memoirs I've read resist dominant interpretations of disability, they also demonstrate the power of formulaic narratives. Despite raising a child with a disability, these parents cannot help but also live, as we all do, within a terrain defined by metaphor. Disability studies scholars have argued that disability is socially constructed. Without denying the reality of bodily impairment, they claim that the disabled experience is shaped and defined in part by the symbolic realm.[12] Parental memoirs provide excellent evidence to support this point, showing how metaphors not only can flatten and devalue their referents but can also invite readers to see in new ways.

Even memoirs that engage in formulaic narratives about disability as a tragic burden do the opposite work as well, offering at least a glimpse into why and how a parent loves this particular child. As they describe in great detail the pleasures and happiness that are part of the family life, they recognize the child as a valuable and loved human being. These memoirs matter because the parental framing and reframing of disability has the potential to instigate significant social change.

In recent history, parental advocacy for the lives of children with cognitive disabilities has had a huge impact.[13] As Michael Bérubé, father of a child with Down syndrome, explains, "In the early 1970s some parents did swim upstream against all they were told and brought their children home, worked with them, held them, provided them physical therapy and 'special learning' environments. These parents are saints and sages. They have, in the broadest sense of the phrase, uplifted the race. In the 10 million-year history of Down syndrome, they've allowed us to believe that we're finally getting somewhere."[14] By recognizing disability in ways different from the "traditional misrepresentations" that Couser refers to, parents have the capacity to change its meaning.[15] Anthropologists Faye Ginsburg and Rayna Rapp identify parental narratives as capable of "meaning-making," while social science scholars Janice McLaughlin, Dan Goodley, Emma Clavering, and Pamela Fisher similarly describe them as "sense making."[16] In the rest of this chapter, I acknowledge where these memoirs buy into prevailing cultural narratives that identify disability with stigma, but I also validate their work to humanize and value the children in these books and to reframe our view of "typical" personhood through the lens of disability.

The genre of memoirs by parents of children with disabilities isn't new: entertainer Dale Evans published a book about her daughter Robin, who had Down syndrome, in 1953.[17] However, we are in the midst of a publishing surge. Of the nineteen full-length, single-authored memoirs I have read, almost all were published since 2000.[18] Most were written by women (although a significant minority—seven—were by men), and gender difference did seem to affect the content and tone of the memoirs. All but one of the books were about children with cognitive disabilities. Six of the memoirs described children with autism, six described children with Down syndrome, and seven were about other disabilities that involved cognitive or intellectual components.

These narratives are particularly significant wherever the children may not ultimately be able to narrate their own lives or consent to their depiction—either because of cognitive disability or because of how young they were when the books were published. The authors share several characteristics: all are white and middle class, and a significant number are professors, although the memoirs themselves are not written as academic studies.[19] Their differences are also significant. Some, such as *The Year My Son and I Were Born: A Story of Down Syndrome, Motherhood, and Self-Discovery*, by Kathryn Lynard Soper, were written with a religious perspective (in this case the Church of Jesus Christ of Latter-Day Saints). Others, such as Richard Galli's *Rescuing Jeffrey*, offer an explicitly rational approach, and still others, such as Beth Kephart's *A Slant of Sun: One Child's Courage*, make use of more explicitly literary framing to present the disability.

Memoirs as Sites of Dehumanization

Sometimes, parental memoirs subtly or overtly dehumanize the child through the portrayal of a family's excessive grief, through troubling comparisons of disabilities, or through a reliance on medical frameworks that make disability seem like an individual affliction in need of correction or cure. Even if the child who is the immediate subject of the book isn't directly dehumanized, a more general stigma may be cast over people with disabilities.

Excessive grief is one of the most obvious features in the parental memoir. The child is a tragedy, a source of almost unbearable sadness. Misery takes up the first half to three-quarters of many such books. They start with a brief period of happiness—often the days before birth or the first days, months, or even years before the disability becomes obvious. Then the story quickly and often dramatically segues to misery. Many narratives grieve the loss of the idealized perfect child who wasn't born, as when Jane Bernstein writes of her blind daughter, "The pictures I did not realize I had created so vividly of my bright, beautiful, healthy daughter are gone. In their place are resurrected memories of every blind person I have ever seen, beggars mostly, blind men with eyes that roll in their sockets that terrified me as a child and terrify me now. My daughter, my child. And there is nothing hopeful I can conjure, nothing at all."[20]

Like Bernstein, other authors express hopelessness at the prospect of their child's disability. Soper, mother of an infant with Down syndrome, reacts to an encouraging conversation with her mother by explaining, "I wanted to join her in that hopeful place where there was nothing to be sad about. I knew it was real. I kept reaching for it within myself, as if reaching for a light switch in a dark room. But all I touched was doubt."[21] Memoirs also describe feelings of ineffectiveness and deficiency, as when Kephart, mother of a child on the autism spectrum, writes, "I scream my helpless anger into an empty room."[22] Later, as the narrative nears its turning point, she explains, "I have to say that it wasn't easy. I have to say that the weeks seemed endless and that friendships dwindled and that what I considered my youth left me. I have to say that there were wars inside me and fists pounded into the bed at night, my whole body furious about what had not been achieved."[23] Kephart confesses that grief turned to isolation, frustration, and rage.

Undeniably, grief is a familiar and understandable part of many parents' discovery that their child has a disability. I experienced a version of this grief, as did most other parents I know who have children with disabilities. Having that heartache narrated in the memoirs is honest; it allows the parents to be fully human instead of paragons of virtue. It serves a literary function in making the parent narrator more sympathetic, complex, and rounded and provides a source of reassurance and identification for parent readers. For instance, one reader wrote in an online review of *Road Map to Holland*, "I received this book yesterday afternoon and finished it today. What can I say—I was completely and utterly entranced by the honesty and realness of what I read. Having a child with DS too, I could feel her pain, feel her raw emotion, feel her fear. But as I turned each page, I felt myself being forgiven along with her, and it's been a long time since I've felt so much relief and joy."[24] Indeed, a number of online comments by readers identify the narration of grief as an important validation and aid to their own healing and family integration.[25]

Sometimes, dwelling on grief can be a more explicit narrative strategy. Jane Bernstein opens *Rachel in the World*, the follow-up memoir to *Loving Rachel*, by noting that narrating her suffering and challenges in her first book was intentional because in the early days of her daughter's life, "I hated the treacly language people often used when writing or speaking about children with 'special needs,' the ruffled, fluffy packaging, the compression and tidying up of a family's disarray into neat, predictable little stages. . . . To me, *Loving Rachel* was grittier and harsher than the books I found on the library shelves."[26] She wrote this way because this level of honesty was what she wanted to read in books.

My point is not, then, that representations of grief are invalid, inaccurate, or hurtful. But when memoirs focus so fully and in such great detail on the grief, it becomes the overriding emotion. When grief so dominates a narrative, it may leave readers with the impression that unhappiness is the primary experience of a family's encounter—or possibly even most families' experience—with disability. As the other epigraph in this chapter asserts, "Parenting a (disabled) child can be tiring, distressing, upsetting and heartbreaking. It can also be rewarding, affirming, enjoyable and heartwarming."[27] The memoirs' elaboration of misery and grief risks focusing too much on the first part of this equation, leaving the reader dwelling on hardship while obscuring the more surprising insight that parenting children with disabilities, much like parenting typical children, is often a source of joy and sustenance. In this way, parent-authors diminish their potential to advocate for a more complex and accurate understanding of life with a disabled child.

To be sure, grief serves a narrative function, setting off a trajectory which—by and large, but not always—ends with the parent-author recognizing and affirming the humanity and other positive characteristics of the child. Indeed, the vast majority of memoirs offer a turning point at which the parent comes to see the falsehood of the societal stereotypes about disability. Sometimes this recognition is explicit; other times more subtle. Some might argue that the heart of the story is the moment when the parents learn they were wrong, and its aftermath. But because this turning point often happens near the end of the book, it cannot lessen the likelihood that much of the reading experience has bolstered negative stereotypes about disability. The unhappiness is the clearest, most fully articulated aspect of some memoirs. The overriding message of these books often seems to be, as Johnson's epigraph might put it, "Thank god you don't have a child with a disability."

By following a trajectory defined by grief, memoirs repeatedly suggest—if not overtly articulate—that the child's main function in the world is to cause pain to the adults around him or her. This dehumanizing trajectory may be subtle, operating via pity, for instance, but some-times it's overt, such as in *This Lovely Life*, by Vicki Forman (2009), the mother of premature twins. The children faced a number of severe med-ical challenges, and one infant died. After Forman shares that her son Evan has a life-threatening heart condition, the author's mother says, "What can I tell you, Vicki. . . . The doctors who resuscitated those ba-bies should be shot. They've left you with a severely disabled child and ruined your life and his. That's all there is to say."[28] Interestingly, Forman doesn't disagree with her mother here or anywhere else in the memoir. Her immediate response is to disagree with the word *disabled*. She ex-plains, "I wanted to say, *You're wrong, he's not severely disabled. Maybe my life is ruined, and maybe his is too. But he is* not *disabled*."[29] In this passage, Forman isn't attempting to correct her previous doubts about her son's humanity. Even as she tells his life story, these doubts create tension by remaining constantly in play. The dehumanizing notion that perhaps Evan's life should have ended—"*Maybe my life is ruined, and maybe his is too*"—is never fully countered. Notably, Forman felt the stigma of the word *disabled* to be so toxic that she couldn't imagine it applying to her son under any circumstances. Thus, instead of rescript-ing the pejorative associations surrounding disability, Forman reinforces them by wanting to deny that they describe her son.

The memoir *Where We Going, Daddy? Life with Two Sons Unlike Any Others*, by Jean-Louis Fournier (2008), is dehumanizing in other ways. Fournier offers a bleakly humorous take on parenting two children with disabilities. The account often comes across as grappling with his per-ception that his sons aren't human. He expresses devastation that they can't read or write and can't have conversations with him. Although he acknowledges things they can do and enjoy (one son loves banging rhythms to songs, for instance, and the other figures out how to lie and manipulate his parents—a significant communicative accomplishment), these achievements are presented as dark comedy. He notes such fam-ily facts as "Our family photo album is flat as a fillet of sole. We don't have many pictures of them, we don't feel like showing them off. Normal children are photographed from every angle, in every pose, on every occasion. . . . They follow their progress step by step. With a handicapped child, no one really feels like following their fall."[30] The parents, then, are suffering so greatly that they can't even document their sons' existence in a photo album or participate in the most mundane of parenting activities.

The book is written as an apology to the sons for bringing them into the world "so wrong."[31] And while Fournier tries to express his love, his subjects come across as two beings who are not people but tragic mistakes. Remarkably, the book received a great deal of praise and attention. *Where We Going, Daddy?* was excerpted by NPR shortly after it was released in the United States, and reviewer Cord Jefferson says Fournier writes "honestly," "admirably," and "bravely": "By the final story, you'll be touched no matter what. But you'll probably also find that you're laughing at things you never thought funny before."[32] As a parent of a child with a disability, I did not find myself laughing at all as I read *Where We Going, Daddy?*

Another way these memoirs struggle with the full humanity of the child is by focusing on a medicalized picture of disability. As disability studies scholars and disability activists have noted, medicine has provided a great deal of valuable help to people with disabilities, but the medical model of disability is inadequate. Simi Linton explains, "The medicalization of disability casts human variation as deviance from the norm, as pathological condition, as deficit, and, significantly, as an individual burden and personal tragedy. Society, in agreeing to assign medical meaning to *disability*, colludes to keep the issue within the purview of the medical establishment, to keep it a personal matter and 'treat' the condition and the person with the condition rather than 'treating' the social processes and policies that constrict disabled people's lives."[33] The medical model is familiar in our culture, and in foregrounding it, parents reinforce the idea that the person with the disability is a problem.

Some memoirs dwell on the complications experienced by the child and emphasize various medical settings. Sometimes the authors appear to strive for neutrality, while other times they are critical, as when Forman describes a hospital where her son Evan has an extended stay as a "Dickensian netherworld."[34]

However, regardless of whether the children have been hospitalized, medical assessment processes, therapeutic procedures, and labeling feature prominently in most of the books I read. These approaches are, of course, a primary way our culture makes sense of disability, and they are often among the only tools available to new parents. Parents are often desperate for a label, and large parts of their stories may retrace efforts to find out "what's wrong" with their child.[35] On the whole, even if the parents have difficulties with, and complaints about, the medical system, these authors rarely expand from their complaints into a broader consideration of the limits of the medical model in accounting for disability.[36]

Disability activists and scholars of disability studies note that the personal difficulties described by parental memoirs are intimately linked with questions about broader cultural attitudes. As disability studies scholar Lennard Davis notes, "The body is never a single physical thing so much as a series of attitudes toward it."[37] In other words, much of the suffering experienced by the families in these books comes from the negative responses of other people. Fournier's book does an excellent job of documenting the failures of an ableist culture. He describes many of his friends' responses to his sons' disabilities as "inanities," but they strike me as outrages.[38] He notes, for instance, friends who told him, "I would have smothered him at birth, like a cat."[39] A close friend who is godfather to his son Thomas began ignoring the boy after learning of his disability.[40] Fournier presents this information fairly flatly, and readers cannot tell how much he disagrees with this treatment or sees it as natural, inevitable, or simply the way things are. He passes by numerous opportunities to criticize those who devalue his sons because of their disabilities. Even when he is critical of his sons' treatment, he fails to present his complaints as part of a broader discounting of people with disabilities. One example is his description of the support braces his sons wear:

> When you pick them up in your arms it feels like you're holding a robot. A metal doll.
>
> It takes a monkey wrench to get them undressed at night. When you peel their breastplates off, you find purple welts left on their naked torsos by the metal stays, and all that's left are two shivering little plucked birds.[41]

This description is Fournier's chance to criticize a culture unable to develop therapeutic prostheses that would actually help and nurture, instead of causing pain and damage to his sons' bodies. Clearly, many of the challenges Fournier and his sons experience are not evidence of the sons' shortcomings but demonstrate society's failure to provide the kinds of support that would allow this family to develop more fully and live out more of their potential. As I'll discuss below, Bérubé and Ralph James Savarese offer counterexamples of parents who use their struggles as an opportunity to indict the broader culture.

Another dehumanizing trend, particularly in memoirs in which the child has autism or other developmental delays that may be challenging to diagnose, is the use of "retardation" as a benchmark. In her 1967 memoir, *The Siege: A Family's Journey into the World of an Autistic Child*, Clara Claiborne Park fears that her daughter Elly would be "retarded," calling this "the very worst possibility."[42] She writes: "I had a horror of retardation. I assumed I could rise to most challenges if my children presented them, but I had wondered about that one. . . . But apparently this was not the worst possibility. There was another. The worst diagnosis he could give us would be a different word altogether—autism."[43] Park uses her fear of Down syndrome to frame the significance of her daughter's autism. If it's worse than "retardation," then it must be really, really bad. As the book progresses, however, she decides that autism is actually preferable to Down syndrome. Describing her daughter's interactions in a special needs preschool, she explains, "She functioned far more ably than the overgrown, affectionate Mongoloid who moved clumsily among the toys. . . . [The students] became contributing members of the school, even if like the little Mongoloid all they could contribute was their helplessness."[44]

Although they may be subtler, some more recent memoirs make similar comparisons. For instance, in the days before she knew her daughter had cognitive disabilities, Jane Bernstein recounts conversations in which "I tell them how I feel I have more to offer to a child who is . . . visually handicapped than I would a child who is retarded (I wouldn't begin to know what to *do* with a retarded child)."[45] So too, Vicki Forman recounts her father saying, as a worst-case scenario, "I don't know, Vicki. . . . The baby might end up with mental retardation. It's possible."[46] In these memoirs, the specter of "mental retardation" keeps appearing as if it's the thing to be most afraid of, the point at which all your hard work has been for nothing, the line past which your child is no longer human. Although Bérubé makes a compelling argument about the toxicity of the word *retarded* (a point many organizations advocate as well), the repeated appearance of this term suggests that authors are either unaware of the offense or are perhaps using it strategically.[47] As recounted earlier, Groneberg, in her moment of self-identified despair, describes herself as "the woman with the retarded son."

Even when it's not used in such a shocking way, retardation (and often specifically Down syndrome) is the measuring stick for other forms of cognitive disability. In *Not Even Wrong: A Father's Journey into the Lost History of Autism* (2004), Paul Collins discusses the "Sally and Anne" test that appears in many memoirs about children with autism. The test assesses a child's ability to think from the perspective of another person. Collins observes, "A typical three-year-old can figure it out, and indeed, in test after test they do figure it out. So, for that matter, can three-year-olds with Down's [sic] syndrome. It's not a hard question. Only . . . the autistic kids keep missing it."[48] The reference to the abilities of a toddler with Down syndrome is a way of indicating the ease of the question, as well as letting the reader know *how bad* it is that Collins's son, who has autism, is unable to answer it.[49] Remarkably, these moments denigrate people with cognitive disabilities to more fully humanize children with other sorts of disabilities. Authors endorse the stigma against cognitive disabilities by saying in essence, "At least my child's not like that," or, "Oh, no—my child might be like that!"

As I've shown, parental memoirs can reinforce familiar, deeply troubling attitudes about people with disabilities as tragic, burdensome, and unworthy. Those narratives can have consequences that extend beyond the boundaries of any given individual's life story, influencing how people with disabilities are seen and understood in the world as citizens and human beings.[50]

Memoirs as Sites of Resistance

We have seen how parental narratives sometimes hijack and undermine the disability rights or disability studies perspective. However, these memoirs can also powerfully combine political and parental functions. As McLaughlin and her co-authors of the excellent *Families Raising Disabled Children* note, "Families are not simply microcosms of society or community: they exist potentially as spaces through which dominant ideas associated with autonomy, choice, individuality and freedom are understood and contested. The family allows a place to work out ways of living, drawing on and challenging ideas about childhood, disability and parenting that exist in the public domain."[51] In other words, while families can and do reflect societal pressures and trends, they also create sites of resistance as they grapple with key ideas about what it means to be a citizen or even a person. Parental memoirs can demonstrate this activist function.

Many people see disability as alien and frightening.[52] Perhaps they recognize, as is often pointed out, that disability can happen to anyone at any time, and it will happen to most of us at some point in our lives. Parental memoirs, then, can offer a different vision of disability, one that is intimate and loving. Philosopher Eva Feder Kittay, for example, explains her relationship with her disabled daughter: "It is because I see Sesha close up, because I have a deep and intimate relationship with her, that I am able to see what is hidden from those who are not privileged enough to see her when she opens up to another. . . . Without a strong affective bond with people with severe cognitive disabilities, we often fail to get a glimpse into the lives of these persons."[53] The genre of the parental memoir has the potential to bridge the intimate and the public, contributing to reworking prevailing perceptions of disability. Parent-authors have the experience and the affection to challenge misinformation. They do so in part by articulating pleasure as a counterpoint to grief, by focusing on disability as a cultural construction rather than as an individual pathology, and by using their own viewpoint as a new lens to see mainstream society. These are all ways of fully humanizing and advocating for people with disabilities.

Some memoirs do a good job of demonstrating that disability arises less from differences of body and mind than from social and environmental barriers. For example, Savarese begins his 2007 book, *Reasonable People: A Memoir of Autism and Adoption*, with an explanation of the cultural work his memoir will do. Aspiring to change medical and popular definitions of autism, he tells his readers, "This book stands in direct opposition to the begrudging appreciation of autistic accomplishment and, even more important, to the notion of 'classical autism' as not affording 'a window' on an Autist's interior. Indeed, it demonstrates just how dynamic and human that interior can be, and it demands that we rethink the 'creature for whom very little future lies in store.'"[54] His book is in no sense grounded in grief, tragedy, or "making do"; instead, it's self-consciously resistant, and he alerts the reader to "the work of activism I wish this book and its author to perform."[55] In this way, Sava-rese leads by recognizing that the parental memoir can make powerful cultural interventions.

In *Not Even Wrong*, Collins offers a different but equally compelling challenge to prevailing cultural understandings of autism. He examines well-known autistic figures, from the "wild boy" to the eccentric art-ist, from the "feeble-minded" hermit to geniuses such as Isaac Newton. Ultimately he argues that the categories of feeble-minded and genius have more to do with perceptions of value and productivity than with individual abilities. People with autism are a diverse group, and all have something worthy to contribute. Of his own son, he writes, "It was blind, brilliant, dumb luck that we had an Isaac Newton who focused on some-thing that other people found important. There are Newtons of refrig-erator parts, Newtons of painted light bulbs, Newtons of train schedules, Newtons of bits of string. Isaac Newton happened to be the Newton of Newtonian physics, and you cannot have him without having the oth-ers, too."[56] Collins identifies what Savarese calls "begrudging apprecia-tion of autistic accomplishment," and he appeals for an acceptance of all people with autism, no matter how impractical their disabilities may be to mainstream society.

Even the less overtly analytical parents, those who are less self-consciously resistant, recognize the power of damaging cultural stereo-types. For instance, in *The Year My Son and I Were Born*, Soper objects to terms like "Down syndrome child" and people who make assump-tions about her son. She's pleased when Thomas defies expectations by screaming at a woman who wants to hold him because "Down's babies [are] always so happy!"[57] She also investigates the constraints that institutionalization created for people with Down syndrome. To-ward the end of the book, she acknowledges that Thomas was limited more by negative perceptions of his potential than by bodily or cogni-tive impairments: "Thomas's diagnosis brought some inherent difficul-ties, like health concerns and education issues, but the stuff that *really* hurt didn't come from Down syndrome. It came from my reaction to Down syndrome. And that reaction was based largely on ignorance and prejudice."[58]

Another contribution parents make to our cultural understanding of disability is to counter grief with joy. Johnson notes that people with disabilities "need to confront the life-killing stereotype that says we're all about suffering. We need to bear witness to our pleasures."[59] Some parental memoirs do this. Take, for instance, this description of a morning in Kittay's home:

> I evoke a morning in my kitchen when Sesha, accompanied by her care-giver, is having breakfast, and I sneak in to give her a kiss:
>
> Sesha, as always, is delighted to see me. Anxious to give me one of her distinctive kisses she tries to grab my hair to pull me to her mouth. Yet at the same time my kisses tickle her and make her giggle too hard to con-centrate on dropping the jam-covered toast before going after my hair. I negotiate, as best I can, the sticky toast, the hair-pulling and raspberry jam-covered mouth. In this charming dance, Sesha and I experience some of our most joyful moments—laughing, ducking, grabbing, kissing.
>
> They are "small" pleasures, to be sure, but pleasures that provide so much of life's meaning and worth that they permit the deep sorrows of Sesha's limitations to recede into a distant place in the mind; they are small joys, but are so profound that they even make me question that very sorrow. It is a pleasure that Sesha and I would have been denied if we could not share our lives together.[60]

Kittay effectively describes the importance of happiness and laughter; such aspects of parenting children with disabilities remain invisible to much of our society. She doesn't invoke this pleasure in an easy, senti-mentalized way to deny the grief or challenges. She acknowledges the "deep sorrows" that are part of life as a parent of a child with disabilities (as is often also true of parenting typical children), but she doesn't allow grief to take the floor. Kittay's daughter is older (in her thirties when the book was published) than the subjects of the other memoirs discussed in this chapter. Decades of experience have distanced Kittay from the initial shock and grief of discovering her daughter's disability and have given her the wisdom of hindsight. She also has full-time caregivers to attend to her daughter's needs. This perspective allows her to describe what might strike many readers as an unusual morning ritual in a way that is clearly affectionate, playful, and funny.

Although descriptions of satisfaction, and even pleasure, are crucial to a revisionist account of parenting children with disabilities, they dominate only a few memoirs I considered. Many of the memoirs I read began by anticipating ambiguity, uncertainty, and pain. Some are subtle, such as *Loving Rachel*, which begins, "It is the kind of summer day that New Jersey is known for, with air that is thick and still unbearably hot." Similarly, the first sentence of *Road Map to Holland* reads, "It's hard to know where to begin." *The Year My Son and I Were Born* offers the clearly negative beginning "No. Oh, no," while *This Lovely Life* starts with "I learned about grief during this time."

By contrast, *Life as We Know It* is filled with such delight that no reader can leave it thinking, "Thank god I don't have a kid with a disability." The author's treatment of parental grief takes up less than five pages. And the book begins with an expression of tenderness rather than foreboding or despair: "My little Jamie loves lists." Of all the memoirs I've read, this book has the most positive introductory sentence, one that conveys love, even adoration. Jamie is unequivocally identified as the author's child and as an individual, not a defect or problem, as in the beginning of many similar narratives. As a parent, I was excited by this opening sentence: I immediately recognized that this book would offer much of the hope, humanization, and validation that I was seeking.

Bérubé writes consistently of the pleasures that come from life with Jamie, as when he describes Jamie and his older brother, Nick, who "was, and still is, his chief cheerleader. Watching his delight in watching Jamie's progress quickly became, for me, one of the primary delights of being alive, and it was clear that Jamie felt more or less the same way. As did Janet."[61] He describes Jamie's slow development as funny and wonderful, without denying the challenges. In comparing Jamie's development with his brother Nick's, Bérubé observes, "Jamie, by contrast, was not only slower but *elaborately* slower."[62] In describing Jamie's efforts to learn to see and grab an object, Bérubé reports that he and Janet referred to him as "world's worst predator."[63] Here Bérubé does not sentimentalize or overly dramatize the challenges facing Jamie and his family. He acknowledges the intense work a child with a disability such as Down syndrome will have to do, but he frames this work not as a cause for parental grief but as a surmountable struggle and sometimes a reason for celebration—and amusement.[64]

The first time I read *Life as We Know It*, I laughed at Jamie's "world's worst predator" moniker, because I had experienced the same phenomenon with my daughter—and because Bérubé recounts it as a family experience, not a tragedy. In *Life as We Know It*, parenting a child with a disability is complex, rich, and far more pleasurable than tragic.

Similarly, Savarese recounts the delights and the difficulties he and his wife experienced in adopting DJ, "the boy who had filled our hearts with love beyond bursting. Picture brightly colored helium balloons painting the horizon, floating above the hills of central Iowa. Can we be this full? Can we go this high?"[65] Raising DJ is challenging, of course, but having him as part of their family is an unadulterated joy. Indeed, several parents describe pleasures that are intimately linked to the challenges they faced with their children. When Kephart's son Jeremy, who is on the autism spectrum, finally learned to speak and describe his world, Kephart found that her son's delays made the accomplishment all the more thrilling: "Talking with Jeremy about the way his mind works became another port of entry. It became some of the most satisfying conversations I will ever have, one of the many privileges I have as a mother to my son."[66]

Similarly, Forman describes the rewards that emerge from her struggles to accept her son's disabilities: "This year, I could begin to see the boy emerging beyond the disabilities. On a cool fall day in my friend Susan's backyard, my son gave me his first smile. It had been nine months since he'd been home, and when I saw his baby gums for the first time, his lips pressed open in a full grin, I cried."[67]

A number of authors relate the simple pleasures of interacting with their children, such as Groneberg's description of bath time: "Avery has taken the little green ninja from Bennett. Avery puts the ninja in the plastic teddy bear and smiles, then laughs. The ninja inside the bear! He lifts it up to show me. Laugh laugh laugh. Avery's laugh makes me laugh, too."[68] It's difficult to find a representative quotation from these passages because they're often describing uneventful, nondramatic moments—and that's the point. These moments aren't offered as explicit challenges to social expectations, but they function in that way, destigmatizing and humanizing the children described.

Most of the memoirs I've read eventually portray children with disabilities as full, significant, and valuable human beings, worthy of love and respect. Toward the end of George & Sam: Two Boys, One Family, and Autism (2004), author Charlotte Moore offers a chapter called "Compensations." Her chapter title is somewhat ambiguous, suggesting, perhaps, that there need to be ways in which parents are repaid for the difficult work of raising children with autism. However, Moore, like other authors, affirms the humanity of her sons by affirming her love for them: "I learned, long ago, that loving children like these had to be unconditional. That's true of loving all children, actually, but with autism you quickly learn that you can't look for gratitude or reciprocity. . . . This wasn't a hard lesson to master. Loving them is the easy part. They're very loveable. Luckily, I'm not the only person who feels this."[69] Moore normalizes the work of being a parent to her children when she writes, "That's true of loving all children." But she also stresses that it is easy to give her sons love because they are "very loveable."

Some memoirs go further, using their child's experiences as a new lens to view the world. If personhood is typically understood in terms of "autonomy, choice, individuality and freedom," these memoirs conceive of it differently.[70] Bérubé does this repeatedly, offering Jamie as a human prototype, a model who helps to illustrate essential human qualities. For instance, he notes, "Jamie would not grow up on his own, any more than you or I did. . . . He would realize his individual potential only by leaning on our mutual human interdependence—just like everyone else, only a bit more so."[71] Similarly, Kittay and the parents interviewed for *Families Raising Disabled Children* insist that interdependence is a universal human condition.[72] Thus, parents can challenge the notion of independence as the defining quality of personhood. They can be part of the disability studies and disability rights efforts to reconsider what it means to be fully human.

These memoirs can also illuminate inequality while pointing the way to a more just society. Savarese uses his son DJ's experience as a case study for our cultural failings. He argues, "We give up on people way too easily—and not just the cognitively disabled, but all sorts of folks, especially children. (Or worse, we never even try to begin with.) 'I dream about life,' DJ says. 'I wonder what i will become of myself.' Surely, a just world would devote itself to equal opportunity dreaming and becoming."[73] Other authors use disability as an opportunity to call for greater compassion, as when Kephart writes, "We are thrown together on a temporary planet, and the only thing we have to protect ourselves from the fury of our fate is kindness incarnate, small acts of grace."[74] Whether framed as compassion or as a more pointed call for a just world, these parental memoirs can—and should—encourage activism.

I am not suggesting that authors should avoid portraying the challenges of parenting a child with a disability. Of course it's hard, as is all parenting. Each child's disability will present its own particular challenges, as may the lack of support and the societal stigma a family has to negotiate. One important role of these memoirs is to articulate struggles that may otherwise be invisible or misunderstood. Nor do I argue that such memoirs must have a happy ending, what Clara Claiborne Park refers to as "the success story everybody wants to hear."[75] Savarese makes a similar point: "The problem with concluding a memoir of disability on a note of triumph is perpetuating the primary cliché of the genre."[76] The success story is as flattening as are many of the other memoirs I've critiqued.

I'm arguing, instead, that these memoirs can and should help rewrite the cultural meanings associated with disability. According to Ginsburg and Rapp,

> The cultural activity of rewriting life stories and kinship narratives around the fact of disability . . . enables families to comprehend (in both senses) this anomalous experience, not only because of the capacity of stories to make meaning but because of their dialogical relationship with larger social arenas. . . . In other words, the way that family members articulate changing experiences and awareness of disability in the domain of kinship not only provides a model for the body politic as a whole but also helps to constitute a broader understanding of citizenship in which disability rights are understood as civil rights.[77]

Parents of children with disabilities are well positioned to challenge the cultural meaning of disability and therefore the broader understanding of citizenship and civic identity. Through their intimate, loving relationships with their children, these parents can develop and communicate a critical stance on mainstream culture's fears and misunderstandings.[78]

At the most fundamental level, these memoirs help make people with disabilities visible *as people*. Parent-memoirists have particular experiences that make them both knowledgeable and compelling narrators. They are allowed to say things that others might not say, to take on the role of observer and critic. They offer an intimate and public articulation of how our culture misrepresents disability. Further, they can describe what it means to view people with disabilities through the perspective of love, hope, high expectations, and positive evaluation. These are perspectives that our culture very much needs to hear.

5

Accessible Words

Alison Piepmeier and the Boundaries of Disability

GEORGE ESTREICH

Though Alison Piepmeier was best known as a feminist literary critic with a strong focus on disability, her academic writing was insufficient to fully demonstrate Alison's range, creativity, and questing mind. Her informal writing—op-eds, articles, and blogs—displayed something else, an essayist's skill with metaphor and narrative, a taste for stylistic experiment, and a drive to connect with readers outside the academy. These talents reached their peak in Alison's blog *Every Little Thing*, which ran from 2013 to 2016 and dealt with the core topics of this book: disability, illness, and motherhood.

Over time, my understanding of the blog has changed radically. While Alison was alive, I read her blog for her voice, her insights, her humor. But I also read it for updates. I wanted to know how she was, and I wanted to know, without asking, about her prognosis. To read it in real time was to follow her story without knowing its end. To read it afterward was utterly different: I began to see it as a single piece of writing.

After Rachel and I took on this project, I reread *Every Little Thing* straight through. I was looking for paragraphs or sentences I could use, possibly even for a personal chapter cobbled together from blog posts and unpublished material. As I read, though, I came to see that plucking paragraphs out of context does Alison a disservice: the writing is already in the context she has chosen.

I later learned that Alison wrote poems in college. This news didn't surprise me: I had come to see her as a creative writer as well as a scholar, talents that she merged in her blog. Though the blog began as a casual home for (as she put it) "random crap," it evolved into something much more: an open-ended digital essay informed by feminist principle and exploring the troubled boundary between disability and disease.

* * *

Whether speaking from a bullhorn or sitting at her desk, whether studying homemade zines of young feminists or decrying the actions of the South Carolina legislature, Alison sought connection. Writing—more broadly, expression—was the beginning of a conversation, a response to something in the world. Alison cared deeply about the final form of her writing: her abundant handwritten notes on manuscript pages bear that out. But the form had a purpose, and that was to connect with like- and unlike-minded people. And so the signature of Alison's writing, either scholarly or informal, was its striking blend of complexity and accessibility. This balance was no accident: Alison believed fiercely in feminist principles and disability justice, and she wanted to spur conversation with as wide an audience as possible. As a result, she published not only with university presses and scholarly journals but also in the *Charleston City Paper*, the *New York Times*, and her blog. (Her voice in those publications was often that of your favorite professor: knowledgeable, clear, warm—the professor you could talk to after class.)

The word *access* has special significance in disability studies and disability rights. It refers, of course, to features of the built environment like curb cuts, elevators, and captions—features that, according to historian of design Bess Williamson, constitute "the most literal form" of access. But these features also embody a vision that is, at its best, both practical and idealistic, where arcane-to-the-able-bodied levels of specification (allowable degrees of incline in a ramp, for instance) are inextricable from the creation of "a more inclusive society with greater opportunities for social and political participation."[1] Alison worked toward a more inclusive society on many fronts, and her blog was one such front: writing about her joys and challenges was a way to help her blog's readers imagine what that society might look like and to suggest how much work remained to be done. It was accessible writing in the service of access.

To call for greater access is to question the unquestioned boundaries of a restrictive world, and for Alison, boundaries were generally things to ignore, step over, redraw, or tear down. She was teacher and activist, scholar and essayist. She read canonical literature and girl zines, feminist theory and romance novels. As a researcher, she crossed disciplinary lines, speaking to geneticists, physicians, and genetic counselors and interviewing women who, faced with a diagnosis of Down syndrome in utero, either terminated or carried to term.

Alison's boundary crossing was fueled by her restless, curious, principled mind, but also by her experience of parenting and disability. That experience tends to redraw conceptual boundaries: though raising a child with a disability is popularly believed to be tragic, it is often joyful; though the condition is understood as abnormal, a parent's experience reframes normality itself. The result, for many of us, is a need for complex self-expression, to find a way of writing that blends the academic and the personal, that allows for questioning, witness, and open-ended exploration. For Alison, her blog was one such form of self-expression, and this book manuscript was another.

Alison defined disability as "an embraceable form of diversity." I assume, as did she, that disability is more than a physical fact: it is produced at the intersection of the body and the world, and observable features like an extra chromosome or restricted growth are the beginning of the story and not the end. As journalist Joseph Shapiro wrote in *No Pity*, for someone in a wheelchair, a city block without curb cuts is an island.[2] Without appropriate forms of support, many people with intellectual disabilities are effectively excluded from the community. But Alison's experience of disability was divided and more complex than most, and that complexity drove the best of her writing. She experienced disability indirectly, as Maybelle's mother, and directly, as a cancer patient. For her, questions of disability were not theoretical, or, rather, theory was grounded in the immediate.

Alison's experience of disability was complex, and it demanded a complex response. To convey its impact and significance, she needed more than the scholar's analytical tools; she needed narrative, image, metaphor, wit. In nonfiction, this latitude of approaches is found in the essay. Though Alison, to my knowledge, never named it as such, I came to see her blog as a long, open-ended personal essay: a heterogeneous form, accessible to varied audiences, and hospitable to both critical and creative approaches.

Alison's instincts were as much an essayist's as a scholar's: the sudden flashes of wit, the impulse toward open-ended inquiry, and the furthering of that inquiry with metaphor, image, and narrative. She grounded her work in the senses, addressing the reader informally and confiding rather than declaiming. And she liked to play with form, thinking about the political implications of the form she had chosen. *Every Little Thing* became a place where Alison could use her whole brain and reflect on her whole life, where personal narrative, feminist analysis, and explorations of disability could be blended either seamlessly or, more often, with the seams deliberately showing.

I.

For Phillip Lopate, the essay is essentially conversational. "Personal essayists converse with the reader," he writes, "because they are already having dialogues and disputes with themselves."[3] Alison had "dialogues and disputes" with herself, and she illuminated these interior conversations to spark a larger conversation in the world.

But to a remarkable extent, *Every Little Thing* is composed of conversations with others, particularly with people whose experiences differed from hers. Alison listened, and talked, across boundaries. She was radically open to the voices of others in a way that many people approve of but that few actually practice. She was open, I think, for many reasons, but one reason might be that people with intellectual disabilities are rarely heard, let alone listened to. There was a connection between the world's accessibility to Maybelle and Alison's making herself accessible to the world, listening to people, even those—or especially those—with whom she disagreed.

On October 11, 2013, Alison described a conversation with a doctor at the Annual Education Meeting of the National Society for Genetic Counselors:

- I'm a huge advocate of abortion rights, but it was a little weird yesterday talking to an MD who performs abortions. Among other things, she said, "This one couple saw that tv show with the kid with mosaicism [*Life Goes On*, with Chris Burke, who *doesn't* have mosaic Down syndrome], and they said, 'Our baby might be nearly normal!' I said no, that's not realistic."
- I didn't let this doctor know that I have a child with Down syndrome because I wanted to hear her real, unfiltered thoughts. And wow, were they troubling. For instance, she was *shocked* that people might adopt a child with Down syndrome. "Maybe it's a psychological thing," she said. "They'll never have an empty nest."
- Believe it or not, she actually told me that all people with Down syndrome get Alzheimer's. First, this isn't true. Second, it's something I criticized in my talk on Wednesday: do we need to be talking about Alzheimer's when a child isn't even born yet?[4]

Alison's scene-with-commentary illuminates the false boundaries inscribed around disability. Down syndrome is falsely equated with Alzheimer's disease. Parents are implied to be mentally unwell: needy, damaged, "a psychological thing."

Bullet points were a staple of Alison's style. Their use is revealing. They were probably generative for her, a way to write quickly, a quick-and-dirty way to give form to her darting intellect. They allowed her a language of impressions, glimpses, and insights; they allowed her swift cuts from one perspective to another; and they freed her from linear narrative. In this case, rather than telling the story of an entire encounter, she breaks out the relevant moments of dialogue to highlight medically ratified misconceptions. But the very fact of a dialogue, with Alison recalling and reflecting—"wow, were they troubling"—suggests two critical points about reproductive technologies: First, in practice, the technologies can constitute a vector for the misconceptions of medical personnel. And second, the decisions themselves are mediated by dialogue. Alison's bullet-pointed conversation contains another conversation—the doctor's dismissal of a prospective mother's troubled hope for almost-normality, a dismissal whose certainty is undercut by the doctor's lack of understanding.

One part of Alison's work was to identify and dissect misconceptions like these; another was to refute them. She does this directly, of course, but she also does so in narrative terms. In the blog, the frequent conversations with Maybelle serve this purpose, highlighting Maybelle's personhood and personality. This one, for example, recounted on May 5, 2013, takes the form of a three-line play, a brief dialogue between Maybelle and Alison that nonetheless has much to say about motherhood, domesticity, and negotiation.

So here's what happens with Maybelle: she gets her waffles drenched in syrup. Not drizzled. Her waffles aren't a dry bread-product with just a bit of syrup flavoring them. They are soaked with Log Cabin. Each bite is heavy and dripping. There's a pool of syrup on her plate when she's finished. A common waffle conversation is

Maybelle: Syrup.

Alison: Full sentence, please.

Maybelle: I want more syrup, please.

And then I comply.[5]

I like the ironies of this compressed moment, focused on the word *comply*: Who's really in charge here? It's a negotiation any parent can identify with, a brief transaction over food. In this case, syrup is traded for language. At the same time, the interaction is specific to Down syndrome: language is both difficult and critical for people with Down syndrome, and requiring a full sentence entails both enforcing a standard and helping a future child fit into the world.

Two conversations, one in bullet points, the other as dialogue: Alison was both deliberate and playful in her choices, thinking about how to tell the story, playing with formal conventions. Appropriately enough for her interest in conversation, Alison's blog is filled with greetings to people as well as things: *Hello, ugly car. Hello, new house. Hello, Society for Disability Studies. Hello, travel, thinking new ways. Hello, possible ways of writing multiple things, with the focus on my book (I love it—I want to write it—I love it).* She hailed friends, including me. She says "Good morning, hair!" and "Good morning, day!" These buoyant greetings show someone who was ready to converse with people and the world and to report on the conversation.

Alison does more than report, however: she reflects on the conversation itself, who is in it, how it works rhetorically, and how it relates to her feminist ideals and her goal of justice for people with disabilities.

* * *

Alison's blog, as its title suggests, is filled with the details of daily life. She pays attention to the little things, even or especially while contemplating larger ones. In 2013, for example, she wrote a post titled "Important Life Truths":

- If you leave wet Cheerios on the floor for three or more days, they become so bonded to the wood that you have to use a strong spatula to release them.

. . .

- Bananas are repulsive, but they're easy to carry to work, so you should eat them.[6]

These are snapshots of domestic life, but they are also parodies of advice about how to live—itself a perennial subject of the essay. Moments like these are reminiscent of Kenkō, the fourteenth-century Japanese Buddhist monk whose *Essays in Idleness* are now considered a forerunner of the modern essay. Kenkō had a keen eye for ordinary absurdities—the ceremonial hats had gotten bigger at court, he reports, and so people had to get new, larger lids for their hatboxes. Or this deadpan advice for living: "You should never put the new antlers of a deer to your nose and smell them. They have little insects that crawl into the nose and devour the brain."[7]

In Alison's "Important Life Truths," the title highlights the incongruity between grand ideals and the actual business of daily living—an incongruity magnified by the use of bullet points, as if these were important action items on a company memo. (Alison was funny, in person and on the page. Her wit comes through in titles like *Bitchmother* and *Unitarian Easter: All of the Fun, None of the Jesus*.)

Essays are often meandering, digressive explorations, but the best essayists know when to explore and when to let a descriptive fragment stand on its own. In context, floor-bonded Cheerios and bananas that you hate but eat anyway resonate with larger themes in the blog, including domesticity and the opposition of health to pleasure. But the paradox of seeing large things through small ones is firmly within the tradition of the essay.

Alison's attention to the details of daily life—food, clothes, appearance, cleaning—also reveals her as an astute social observer. Her bemused takes on fashion are woven throughout the blog: Alison's friends trying to dress her in something besides slacks and a Star Wars T-shirt,

Alison mystified as to why she should care. In February 2013, for example, she reflects on a pair of shoes. She is going to a party, and a student suggests different shoes from the ones she has bought. She takes a picture of them and writes, "I'm not opposed to those shoes. I just don't understand them. So, they're cute apparently, but I have no means of assessing them. I suspect I'd look ridiculous in them—but maybe I'm going to look ridiculous in the other ones."[8]

Another, lesser writer might have stuck with ironic distance, wearing a Star Wars shirt with pride, expressing contempt for people who care about how they look. Alison's approach is far more interesting: she combines immersion and distance while suspending judgment. She is open to the experience of enjoying a particular pair of shoes, is willing to try them out, but just doesn't see the point. In a similar post, she narrates being taken to Sexy Siren Aerobics, where she has a good time but finds the experience completely ridiculous. There's a surprising parallel, in fact, between Alison's approach to Sexy Siren Aerobics and her approach to the Annual Education Conference of the National Society of Genetic Counselors: as an outsider, she's open to a new experience, open to the possibility of good people, ready to engage, but at the same time, she is conscious of the inherent absurdities. Even in irony, she did not hold herself apart.

Alison's openness entails contradiction—and, like many essayists, Alison is more interested in distilling contradiction than in resolving it. In this post from February 13, 2014 ("Alison's New Hair"), we find Alison trying to get a good haircut before the "Yes, I'm a Feminist!" party:

> This morning I called the salon and discovered that the *only* time I could get a Ouidad haircut before Feb. 25—the date of Charleston's best feminist party ever—was this afternoon. So I texted Maybelle's favorite babysitter at the very last minute (not that unusual for me, really) and had to admit to her that she'd be hanging with Maybelle so that I could succumb to the white supremacist capitalist patriarchy.
>
> I actually think this may be the best haircut yet.

Moments like these exemplify Lopate's point that essayists turn a private conversation into a public one. From early 2014 on, Alison's conversation was increasingly about illness and disability. Faced with the return of her cancer—and its disabling effects—she responded with imagination, marshaling the themes and techniques of the blog to explore the troubled boundary between disability and disease.

II.

Throughout *Every Little Thing*, cancer and Down syndrome are conceptually distinct. One is a disease, something to treat and cure; the other is a disability, "an embraceable form of diversity," and Maybelle was the one she embraced. In a society where disability is too often medicalized, Alison stood up for a broader, more accepting view, distinguishing the diverse human bodies we welcome from the diseases we seek to cure.

In the blog, Alison embodied this distinction in memorable, ordinary details. Disability was Down syndrome, Maybelle, the breakfast table, an embraceable form of diversity, home. Disease was cancer, fatigue, the enemy of life and hope, the anti-home. On the one hand, there were butter twists from Ralph's Donut Shop, a simple evening reading to Maybelle, a canoe outing with Brian. On the other hand were the exhaustion and nausea of chemo, an insensitive doctor, the loathed smell of antiseptic soap. One set of details brought her to the welcome table of love, companionship, motherhood, connection with others, and new ways of thinking about people. The other divided her from life and pleasure and from the ability to express herself.

Reading the comments on Alison's blog and on Facebook threads discussing the blogs, I was happy to see a total absence of confusion: Nobody got disease and disability mixed up. Everyone treasured Maybelle as a person, honored her as a person in relation to family and community, an individual; everyone wished Alison's glioblastoma gone.

It would have been perfectly understandable if Alison had simply sketched the extremes that we, the readers, assented to. But in typical fashion, Alison questioned even this distinction, finding the places where the boundary between disability and disease was porous and uncertain. (As the disability theorist G. Thomas Couser writes, "The border between disability and illness is not always clear."[9] Illness can cause disability. Some conditions, like chronic pain, can be placed in either category, or both.)

Alison's exploration of the boundary between disability and disease was rooted in intellectual honesty. She believed that writing needed to be equal to the world's complexity. She declared what amounts to an aesthetic: "Complexity, as we all know, is a crucial element of critical thinking and of provocative, substantive writing."[10] So it is no surprise that she lives up to that aesthetic in *Every Little Thing*. But her exploration was also driven by personal experience. Alison was the mother of a girl with Down syndrome; she also had brain cancer. These two radically different conditions converged on the question of independence. In very different ways, Maybelle and Alison were rendered partly dependent on others, and Alison wrote searchingly about this topic, exploring her own contradictions.

It's almost an article of faith in disability studies that pure independence is a fiction. We are interdependent: we rely on one another. Alison argued for this view, and yet, faced with seizures that kept her from driving, she chafed at her loss of independence. What resulted was an inner dialogue, a private conversation that she made eloquently public. Alison posted a raw, self-interrogating meditation on her blog:

> There's a very good chance that I'll never be able to drive again.
>
> I'll never be able to drive again.
>
> It almost makes me tear up to write that, sitting here in the lobby of the Greyhound station. I haven't written much here about my seizures. I haven't written about them as a disability, even though they clearly are

disabling. I am a person who studies disabilities in great depth. It's the focus of my scholarship, and I do a fair amount of activism around it, too. So why don't I want to acknowledge my own disability?

Fear, I think. And ego. Fear because the seizures are connected to the brain tumor, and the brain tumor is connected to my mortality. Fear because I don't want them to get worse and force me to reimagine my professional and personal life. Ego because I want to be a person who drives. "I'm not the kind of person who rides a bus," my ego announces. "It's unacceptable!" I feel ashamed to be a person who has to take cabs, or ride a Greyhound. Flying is, of course, perfectly acceptable, as is taking a cab to the airport. Those things can almost be prestigious, so I have no weird feelings there. But not being able to drive to the grocery store, or the bank, or a speaking engagement a few hours away, feels shameful. It's class based, of course, and based on my desire for "independence," for the ability to control my own movements.

I get that this is troubling, irrational, contradictory to some of my deeply held beliefs about accessibility, identity, and human value. *I get it. I'm not defending this!*

But I'm feeling it. And now I'm writing about it. First time, right? Here I am, feminist disability studies scholar, discussing my own disability. Discussing my fucked up conflicts, conflicts I'm going to need to address.[11]

Every Little Thing is filled with conversations, but here the conversation is internal, the inner dialogue literal: the ego, personified, "speaks." (This is a paradoxical move: Alison both owns a distasteful sentiment and distances herself from it, as if her feelings were both her own and not her own.) And as always, Alison's reflections are vividly anchored to place: reflecting on the body, Alison insists on embodied experience, locating us in "the Greyhound station." She connects driving not to the abstract concept of mobility but to "the grocery store, or the bank, or a speaking engagement." In other words, driving is linked not only to independence in general but also to Alison's domestic and professional life.

On June 25, 2014, Alison provided an update: her neurologist cleared her to drive. (She celebrated this milestone by acquiring a PT Cruiser, which she immediately plastered with feminist bumper stickers.) Though it's been only three months since her post from the Greyhound station, she has come to accept that she does have a disability, that she does depend on others:

> Driving a car doesn't make me think that I don't have a brain tumor. It hasn't allowed me to trick myself into thinking I'm a person who doesn't have seizures—and who might never have big ones again. I'm a person with a disability. I'm a person who has seizures, and a brain tumor. This is something I'm grappling with and that I know I'll be writing more about.
>
> So this is what I think might be happening: I couldn't (can't?) recognize my disabilities. And as a partial result of that, I haven't been able to recognize my fears, my limitations, when I'm in the midst of them. For the last three years I often felt anxious, sad, exhausted being a person who can't do many, many things without the help and support of friends. But I didn't know the depth of those feelings.

This acceptance, though nuanced and partial, produces a transcendent moment of respite:

> Right now the feelings are diminished, and the sense of lightness this brings to my body—like I'm full of oxygen, I'm shining through every pore—is allowing me something new. At some level I'm afraid that this won't last—now that I know what it means, it will be so painful to lose it. But there's no way to know, so I'm trying to be in the present moment.
>
> As I said in the City Paper column, Hello, ugly car. Welcome to the family.

Here, we see Alison's habit of greeting—"Hello, ugly car." But we also see her talent for figurative speech: "I'm full of oxygen, I'm shining through every pore." Alison was ill, but her language is radiantly alive.

From mid-2014 on, the blog focuses increasingly on these moments of peace. The condition that makes her intensely aware of time passing makes it difficult for her to enjoy each moment. So she values, and shares, the moments of pure pleasure when she is able to "be fully present." I see these moments as extensions of Alison's meditations on the idea of home. They are typically described in the company of loved ones—and food. But they broaden "home" beyond the literal, showing us Alison at home in time, at home in her body.

On August 22, 2014, she described getting cinnamon rolls with her mom only a week after surgery:

> As we took this picture of ourselves, I realized that it's been more than a week since I've had a moment like this: sitting in a pastry/coffee shop, having a cinnamon roll ourselves as we waited for it to be time to head back to school. It felt like a new kind of real life, like, "OH, right—this is the sort of thing my life can look like!"

On March 1, 2015, she described a moment with her partner (and soon-to-be husband) Brian at a barbecue restaurant:

> Ultimately, as I sat there with a barbecue sandwich, I felt myself somehow calm down and let the cells go. They aren't all going to go away—all the oncologists have said this—so I want them to lie down, drifting. Some are just shrunk and out of energy. They don't require me to be a warrior—they just need to be allowed to disappear as I do the things that are part of my medical process.
>
> I don't want my body to be a space of domination, a space where I imagine myself as fierce. Instead, I want to be soothing to myself. I want to breathe.

Again we see Alison's talent for metaphor, used to convey the complexities of interior life. We've already seen the way she ascribes unwanted thoughts about disability to "ego," both claiming and rejecting them. Here, something similar and almost shocking occurs. She declines to be at war, to be "a space of domination," and so her account of her cancer cells is almost autobiographical: she associates them with exhaustion and wishes them the peace she wishes for herself. "They aren't all going to go away—all the oncologists have said this—so I want them to lie down, drifting. Some are just shrunk and out of energy." She conveys a difficult, partial acceptance.

But this metaphor also has a social dimension. With it, Alison is responding to blog comments urging her to "fight cancer." Gently but firmly, she rejects this framing: "Other people do find this approach—the attack on the tumor—to be satisfying at multiple levels, so I'm not saying that these loving statements are in any way troubling or inappropriate. They just aren't for me. They aren't what I want, what I need." With these words, Alison both dissects a problematic metaphor and replaces it with a better one. That she *could* do so shows the range of her talents, but it also shows a principled wish to do more than criticize, to offer a positive alternative, to guide and advance the conversation. To do so, Alison not only depends on her skill with words but also exploits the interactivity the online format permits. "Conversation" here is literal, not an academic metaphor.

These moments of respite, with Maybelle, with Brian, with Alison's mother, are moments of feeling at home in the world. More than any literal place, *home* stands for connection: what Alison called "the welcome table," the place where we sit down together. And its opposite is the denial of connection. What matters most are the relationships that sustain us, wherever they occur. Those relationships are constituted, in part, by conversation. Alison's blog, then, was a way of bearing witness to the relationships that mattered to her while reaching out to new people.

For Alison, the act of writing also helped her achieve these moments of being at home in the world. Writing was a way to embrace and resist time's passing. She makes this explicit in a late post titled "Everything Has Changed": "I'm writing because writing gives me a space, a space where I have a moment to reflect." As Brian points out in an essay published after Alison's death, time and mortality were at the core of everything Alison did. She was always writing, because she knew that her time was probably limited. But this awareness lent her writing both urgency and vitality.

Though I see *Every Little Thing* as an extended essay, it is also akin to other artwork governed by arbitrary formal constraints. I think of A. R. Ammons's *Tape for the Turn of the Year*, a long diaristic poem written on an adding-machine tape, which ended when the tape ran out, and an early performance piece by Laurie Anderson, who stood on a block of ice wearing ice skates and playing a violin until the ice melted. Alison's blog matched the arc of her life, and because she was open about the fact of her cancer, you knew, reading her writing, that the tape was finite, that the block of ice was melting and that she was typing away and making music anyhow.

III.

The boundary between disease and disability is troubled by the question of independence and by language itself. Down syndrome and cancer, though radically different conditions, affect both language and cognition. For Alison, Maybelle was fine just as she was, challenges with words and all. And yet, as a writer and scholar, Alison fiercely resisted her own loss of language. As a result, she faced—with rare honesty—a difficult question: what did it mean, on the one hand, to say that one can be fully human despite the impairment of language, while on the other hand, to grieve one's own impairment? The conundrum was complicated by the fact that the loss of language might result not from cancer but from its treatment. In an impossible choice—what Alison would have called *zugzwang*—she had to set life against language.

On August 3, 2014, Alison wrote that the tumor was growing again, that an operation was imminent, and that the tumor was "in the language center of my brain":

> I asked my uncle how I decide: if I allow the neurosurgeon to take out more of the tumor, I'll live longer, and I'll lose language ability—ability that in many ways defines who I am. How do I choose? My uncle said, "You don't choose. You'll get both—language and being alive." I heard what he said. I wrote it down.
>
> And this is still prowling around inside me, a question of my priorities. My #1 priority, which I can recognize with no ambivalence, is being alive for Maybelle. But language—talking, writing, thinking, being outraged, being passionate, being curious, being able to connect with the people I love—is a significant second priority. So important that it's a millimeter below priority #1.

In the early months of the blog, Alison established a style, a distinctive set of concerns and formal features. In the late months of the blog, she adapted that style to the increasingly urgent questions of disability and illness. On December 16, 2015, she wrote about chemotherapy ("Oh, How I Hate the IV Infusion"). The madeleine of memory, here, is the smell of antiseptic soap, which reminds her of the time when Maybelle was in the NICU for a week after she was born. Maybelle was there "only because they were concerned that she had Down syndrome. There wasn't anything other than that. After we discovered her fantastic pediatrician, he said that what she needed was time outside every day." Using bullet points, Alison links this medical treatment to her own:

- It can take forever for the medicine to be delivered. Once in the last month, it took two hours for them to even bring the medicine for the IV infusion. I sat in the chair, plugged into everything, but doing nothing. For an extra two hours.

- That sucks.
- I'm sitting here right now, getting some prophylactic medication for diarrhea/nausea/agony—that's a good thing, actually, not one that I hate—and the nurse just discovered that it's actually going to take longer than she thought, because the doctor wanted to see how much I weigh. I was 139 pounds a few weeks ago. Now I'm back at 149—which is very good, because it means I'm moving back to the normal weight of my body (155 since I was in grad school). She discovered that we're going to have to wait some more, because my weight change required a revision in my dosage.
- What the hell!
- Now I'm home. I'm exhausted—falling asleep—but I wish I could take a shower and throw all my clothes in the laundry. I'm too tired for that right now, but the smell of my clothing is hard to take when the clothing is so near to me. The smell is the first item on my list of things I hate about IV infusion.
- Breaking my heart sometimes.

Alison's use of bullet points seems to express a paradox. She clearly likes their punchy, organized approach: she wanted to get things done. (Note her impatience with waiting for chemo.) And yet she understands that life is not a memorandum or a to-do list and therefore cannot be contained. Still, the form is perfect for the rich inner life of a nonlinear thinker. For a person with an active mind, showing up for chemo, memories of your daughter's time in the hospital, and thinking about cancer's meaning *are* the to-do list. She expresses all this not through formal argument but by playing with form. That play is deadly serious, a necessary labor: Alison describes herself as too tired to take a shower and to throw clothes in the laundry, but she is not too tired to write.

Some of Alison's best writing occurs late in the blog, as she resists the loss of language—and, somehow, turns that deficit against itself:

- Here's an awful change: I couldn't remember Maybelle's name twice recently. Couldn't remember. May . . . Mother fuck. My daughter.

This is a deft, imaginative moment. The post is compressed and moving: Alison ably dramatizes the loss of ability and remembers a gap in memory, using words to evoke the loss of words. Her profanity is also a play on words. The ellipses, a scholar's punctuation, stand for absence.

On March 30, 2016, Alison wrote a post titled "Changing My Body Would help and Terrified Me." One of the most significant parts of the post is the introductory note, where Alison says that she has deliberately left errors in place (another literary experiment) and has sought some editing help:

Preface: What is written below is the result of my challenges with language. Brian did some minimal editing, but you will see some evidence of the problems I am experiencing.

In this note, Alison becomes her own editor, a scholar of her own essay. In doing so, she makes an essayistic choice, a surprising and expressive formal move. At the same time, by emphasizing that she received editorial help, she shows that interdependence is part of life. Even with her language impaired, even in the throes of illness and extreme stress, Alison is thinking as a creative writer: questioning the boundaries of disability, giving us access to her experience. In this way, she advances the conversation. My hope is that the conversation will continue.

6

Six Questions on the Special, the Inclusive, and the Universal

RACHEL ADAMS

Dear Alison,

Since we had a friendship that began and ended with letters, a letter seems like an ideal form for my contribution to your book, which is intended to continue some of the conversations started by your written work, as well as our personal conversations. A letter is, by definition, an open form, one shaped to create dialogue rather than pronouncement and one that imagines being read and responded to. This form is perfectly suited to your temperament as a writer and an activist. When you gave talks and presentations, your responses were so genuine that questions and comments from the audience often turned into dialogue. You loved blogging and journalistic writing because of the wide readerships these forms made available. Your style felt spontaneous and exploratory, making your work accessible outside narrower academic communities. Unlike so many writers, you read and thought deeply about your readers' comments. You were willing to be vulnerable and to change your mind.

This letter is also for me. Isn't the purpose of letters to the dead really to sustain the living? In writing, I can extend the conversations that were central to our friendship and the commitments underlying your work.

The first email came on February 14, 2011. "My name is Alison Piepmeier, and I'm a fan of your work," it began. Blunt and generous, that was vintage Alison. You told me how disappointed you were to miss a panel I was organizing on parenting and disability. Then you went on to tell me about yourself:

> While most of my work until now has centered on contemporary feminism, I've begun feminist disability studies research, and I'm planning to spend the summer digging into the issue of prenatal testing. I have a two-year-old daughter, Maybelle, who has Down syndrome, and that's brought disability onto my radar in a new way. This is the main reason I'm emailing you: since we're both coming at disability from an interdisciplinary, but humanities-based, background, and since we're both feminist scholars with children with Down syndrome, I thought it might be good for us to know each other. In particular, I'd love to know if you're doing research into prenatal testing.

A quick Google search suggested that you were a kindred spirit: a women's studies professor at the College of Charleston and a parent of a child with Down syndrome. You described your occupation as "professional feminist" and your job as "working to bring down the patriarchy." You wore glasses and had wild curls, just like me! You were a prolific and popular blogger, as well as writing journalism and academic essays. I responded right away, thrilled at the connection I felt with you and your work. An excited back-and-forth ensued. I enthused about your blog: "It's always remarkable to me, when I read about other people's experiences, to find such an immediate sense of familiarity and kinship." Over email, we discussed so many things, including school placements, prenatal testing, mutual friends, how to deal with hate mail, and current events. By the time we met in person, I had written, gushingly, "I feel like we're good friends already."

You were always deeply attuned to current events, writing about them through the lens of feminism, social justice, and disability rights. In the past few years, so much has happened that I've wanted to discuss with you. I'm structuring this letter as a series of questions I wish I could ask you.

As your work moved toward ethnography—some of your interviews with women who had undergone prenatal testing and parents of people with Down syndrome are represented in this book—you understood the value of open questions, active listening, and dialogue. In your work, the question is a feminist form, inviting the interlocutor to speak and to be heard without judgment or recrimination, an acknowledgment that they had something to contribute. As the interviewer, you always situated yourself as a participant in those conversations, not as an impartial collector of data but as a stakeholder with your own beliefs and commitments. I write what follows in that spirit. I don't presume to know what your answers would be, but speculating on what you would have found interesting or valuable is a way of keeping our conversation going and drawing attention to the ongoing relevance of the subjects you cover in this book.

What would you make of such recent developments in genomics as the commercialization of prenatal genetic tests, direct-to-consumer genetic services, and the revolutionary gene-editing technology, CRISPR-Cas9? Some of these developments were on the horizon when you started work on this book; others would still have seemed like science fiction. I think these innovations would have interested you, given your concern with the misguided forms of biological determinism that can accompany prenatal genetic testing. By the time of your death in 2016, commercial direct-to-consumer genetic tests had been around for almost a decade. Although the new industry hit some bumps in the road toward US Food and Drug Administration approval, companies like 23andMe, Futura Genetics, and Navigenics now offer tests for genes linked to diseases like celiac, Alzheimer's, and Parkinson's. Other companies test for genes that control receptiveness to medications or indicate whether you are a carrier for inherited conditions like sickle cell disease, cystic fibrosis, or hearing loss, and some firms provide consumers with raw data for the entire genome.[1]

The craze for genetic ancestry testing continues, as do debates about how, and if, genes are linked to social understandings of race.[2] The title of a 2018 story in the *New York Times Magazine* points to the complications these tests are posing to our conventional understanding of identity: "Sigrid Johnson Was Black. A DNA Test Said She Wasn't."[3] The article covers developments in technology, marketing, and the regulation of genetic ancestry tests and includes many firsthand accounts of consumers whose sense of self and family was upended by the results of a genetic test. Many people were left struggling to navigate between a lifelong identity defined by tradition, experience, and family stories and a genetic sequence that indicated unexpected belonging or exclusion.

When my son, Henry, was born with Down syndrome (about a year before your daughter, Maybelle, was born), prenatal screening and, in some cases, genetic testing like amniocentesis and chorionic villus sampling were already a routine part of maternal care. But today, prenatal genetic testing has become big business. Pharmaceutical companies like Natera, Sequenom, and Progenity seek name recognition through advertising and promotional campaigns. When I spent a day shadowing staff at a genetic counseling clinic, I observed at least two brands of tests on the shelves. The group spent the lunch hour listening to a presentation by a lab representative claiming to offer faster and more complete results than those from other labs. When I asked how the counselors chose between one box and another, they told me there was little difference beyond brand names.

Much of the marketing of these products is geared toward genetic counselors, but some of it is also directed at consumers. "Prepare for life," says a large banner across the home page of the Progenity website, superimposed over a changing sequence of videos of happy parents and children, "because it's your future and your family."[4] Some advocates worry that, through advertising, corporations are determining the messaging around the meaning and purpose of prenatal genetic testing and the conditions it is designed to detect. The Progenity ad, for example, equates prenatal genetic tests with planning for future health and happiness, without mentioning the possibility of unwanted results or the limits of what genetic data can predict. Nowhere in these advertisements do we hear the voices of people with genetic disabilities or their families.

In the realm of what once seemed like science fiction, researchers developed CRISPR, a technology that allows for faster, cheaper, and more precise gene editing than was ever available before. CRISPR has been hailed as having revolutionary implications for agriculture, pest control, and human health. But ethicists have advised caution, recognizing the potential for human enhancement and, because the changes are heritable, for unleashing unpredictable consequences on future generations.[5] Despite these warnings, in November 2018, Chinese scientist He Jiankui shocked the world with news that he had delivered the first genetically edited twin babies. A third baby, also bearing genes He edited by CRISPR, was born with little fanfare in January 2020. Although the majority of the scientific community has been critical of He's work, his accomplishment opens the way to future gene-editing experiments on human subjects. Both George and I have written about the ethical dilemmas raised by He's work. George has explored how they are magnified by social media and persuasive rhetoric to make the rogue experiment seem welcome and beneficial.[6] I have argued that the media spotlight on He, dubbed the "Chinese Frankenstein," overlooks the key role mothers continue to play in human reproduction and development.[7]

Like George, you recognized that genetic technology and marketing are closely related to your concerns with disability, identity, and social justice. How would you make sense of these new developments? You might recognize that the ongoing popularization of genetic ancestry tests can create a sense of diversity and interconnection. A. J. Jacobs's book *It's All Relative* argues that combining genetic data with more traditional genealogy can be a force for positive change. The more we know about our heritage, the more we open up unexpected kinship connections that remind us of our shared humanity.[8]

But ancestry testing also has a darker side. I've already pointed out how some consumers have been shocked by results that complicate their understanding of self and family history, but these tests have also been used by white supremacists to establish untainted heritage (with unwanted results dismissed as flaws in the technology).[9] Many of the deterministic beliefs driving the craze for biological ancestry do not bode well for people with disabilities, especially disabilities that have a genetic basis. This focus on genetic ancestry signals a general trend toward the geneticization of culture, a simplified understanding of genes as determinants of identity, behavior, and personality.

Your writing did so much to challenge this view by showing Down syndrome as only one aspect of Maybelle's identity. People with Down syndrome, like all other people, are embedded in kinship networks that shape their personalities and desires in concert with their genes. Knowing your genes means knowing only one aspect of who you are. But as companies like 23andMe expand their services beyond genealogy to health, we can expect an ongoing stream of messaging that equates good genes with happiness, security, and well-being and equates genetic data with reassurance, predictability, and precision.

A technology like CRISPR raises the hopeful possibility of editing away not only genetically based diseases but also genetic disabilities such as achondroplasia, deafness, and Down syndrome; the technology also raises the prospect of selecting for desired traits. Given the present inequalities in healthcare, this technological potential doesn't mean that unwanted conditions would go away. Instead, it means that they would increasingly be seen as a choice or would be concentrated among populations lacking adequate medical care.[10] And as big pharmaceutical companies control the messages around the meaning and purpose of genetic information, they also get to decide which disabilities are bad enough to test for. The wide availability of prenatal genetic tests for Down syndrome, which gives its name to the MaterniT21 test, in itself says something about the severity and undesirability of the condition.

What would you think about ongoing efforts to link the expansion of disability rights with rolling back legalized abortion? One great accomplishment of your work was how effectively it walked the fraught line between justice for people with disabilities and support for women's reproductive rights. I'm sure you would be concerned by the way conservatives continue to use disability to curtail women's reproductive freedom. You wrote with honesty and purpose about your own decisions to terminate unwanted pregnancies in the past. Access to safe and legal abortions by no means changed your commitment to having Maybelle; you very much wanted this pregnancy even after you learned she might have Down syndrome. I shared your outrage over North Dakota's attempt to outlaw abortion after a prenatal diagnosis of a genetic disability; you wrote about the issue in a fine essay in the *New York Times*.[11] Unfortunately, North Dakota was just the first in a growing number of states (e.g., Indiana, Ohio, Louisiana, and Utah) that have enacted similar laws. Now that Justice Brett Kavanaugh has been confirmed, we cannot look to the Supreme Court to uphold the right to safe and legal abortion guaranteed by *Roe v. Wade*, and we can expect the continued false opposition between the rights of women and people with disabilities.

Given your commitment to feminism, how would you describe the role of disability in the #MeToo movement? You wrote passionately about gender oppression and affirmed women's efforts to speak out against injustice of all kinds. I think you would be thrilled at how women have used social media to share stories and build a movement against sexual misconduct. You would applaud the new atmosphere of seriousness and compassion that accompanies their accusations. But you would probably also recognize how people with disabilities have been left on the sidelines, as they have been by so many other movements for social justice. Although women with disabilities are far more likely to be victims of sexual assault and gender-based violence, many have written about feeling marginalized in the #MeToo movement.[12] As with other movements organized around self-expression and finding a voice, #MeToo has not fully recognized the difficulties of including those who do not have the capacity for self-representation. A striking example came to light in January 2019, when an Arizona woman who had been in a vegetative state for over a decade gave birth.[13] Her story draws attention to the violence and sexual abuse that is pervasive in long-term care facilities and among those who do not have access to speech.[14]

People with intellectual disabilities, one of your primary areas of concern, are especially vulnerable. In January 2018, journalist Joseph Shapiro produced a series on the epidemic of sexual assault against people with intellectual disabilities. He quotes US Department of Justice statistician Erica Harrell, who reports that people with intellectual disabilities are seven times more likely to be sexually assaulted by caregivers, staff, or other people with these disabilities.[15] They are also less likely to be able to communicate their desires and needs, to remember or speak accurately about what happened to them, and to be believed, and the perpetrators are less likely to be prosecuted. Because people with intellectual disabilities are often infantilized, their sexuality is not recognized. They receive inadequate education about consent and sexual safety, and their sexual health is neglected.[16] One way of continuing your work at the intersection of feminism and disability studies is to call attention to these problems and to identify creative solutions for them. Shapiro provides a good example in the sexual health curriculum used by Momentum, a Maine agency for adults with intellectual disabilities.[17]

How would the emphasis of your thinking about disability justice have evolved as Maybelle grew up? What would you have said about the challenges facing teens and adults with intellectual disabilities? Your best insights, and your best essays, grew out of experiential knowledge. You wrote powerfully about your experiences of gender, illness, and parenting a disabled child. Most of your writing about disability centered on the issues arising in the first decade of life: family, the ethics and politics of prenatal genetic testing and diagnosis, reproductive freedom, the friendship and support of other parents, play and domestic life, and pre-school and elementary education. Your conversations with Emily Perl Kingsley, Nancy Brown, and other parents of older children with Down syndrome showed your growing interest in the new questions that arise with adolescence and adulthood.

For example, people with intellectual disabilities often have sexual desires and needs that may go unmet because of inadequate sexual education and health care, scant opportunities to meet sexual partners, and lack of privacy. While #MeToo emphasizes vulnerability, people with intellectual disabilities are also likely to experience loneliness, isolation, and frustration caused by a general lack of intimacy in their lives.[18] I've written about how films like *Yo, También*; *Girlfriend*; and *Monica and David* spotlight the desire and sexual agency of adults with Down syndrome and the frustrations that arise from misunderstanding, prejudice, and material circumstances such as educational, housing, and social barriers.[19] I think you would agree that the long-term well-being of people with intellectual disabilities requires finding an appropriate balance between protection from harm and allowing the *right to risk*—the chance to make autonomous decisions, even when they may be risky or unwise—enjoyed by other adults.[20]

You would also have recognized that the need to navigate between sheltering and encouraging independence in people with intellectual disabilities is not limited to matters of sexuality. You would appreciate recent films that have explored the challenges and opportunities of independence for young adults with intellectual disabilities. Charlotte Glynn's 2009 documentary film *Rachel Is* follows Jane Bernstein as she struggles to find appropriate housing for her daughter, Rachel, a woman with intellectual disabilities. Both mother and daughter are desperate for Rachel to move out of her childhood home but are stymied by how hard it is to find a place where she will be safe, happy, and respected. Dan Habib's 2018 film, *Intelligent Lives*, which follows three young adults with intellectual disabilities at crucial points of transition, also focuses on the

challenges of independence in work, high school, and college gradua-
tion. And a film based on Andrew Solomon's book *Far from the Tree*
shows how Jason Kingsley, a man with Down syndrome and someone
you interviewed for this book, has (with the help of his mother, Emily
Perl Kingsley) made a home with two other friends who enjoy considerable independence but also the supervision of staff.

As someone passionately committed to your career, you would also
have had more to say about the centrality of work to debates about well-
being for people with disabilities.[21] In the United States and the rest of
the world, the statistics for people with disabilities are grim, since the
percentage of these people who are unemployed, living in poverty, or
both is well above national or worldwide averages.[22] Naomi Monplaisir,
one of the protagonists of *Intelligent Lives*, attended a segregated special
education school that exploited students by forcing them to work for
little or no pay. By the time she appears in the film, she has enrolled in
a legitimate job training program and eventually finds employment at
a beauty salon, where she is appreciated and welcomed. But such opportunities are not appropriate for everyone. Jane Bernstein, the mother
featured in *Rachel Is*, has written in defense of sheltered workshops that
are being shut down across the country. These programs have been
controversial among disability advocates because they pay participants
below minimum wage, but Bernstein argues that they give a sense of
purpose to her daughter, who is unlikely to succeed in a conventional
workplace. While closing the workshops may benefit some individuals
who can make the transition into the regular workforce, Bernstein worries that people like her daughter will suffer.[23]

Work is not an option for all people with disabilities. Another pro-
tagonist of *Intelligent Lives* is Naieer Shaheed, a talented artist on the
autism spectrum. The film shows him exploring, with the support of
his parents and art teacher, art programs to attend after graduating
from high school. Concerned about how easily a tall black man with
erratic behavior could become a target of violence, Naieer's parents ex-

press their desire to see him in an environment that is safe but that also nurtures his creativity. Alison, you would be thrilled to hear about the artistic successes of some people with Down syndrome you know. In summer 2018, Jamie Bérubé was part of an exhibition at the LAND Studio & Gallery in New York City, where his remarkable drawings of colored DNA-like ladders sold out. More of his pieces appeared in an exhibit at the Snug Harbor Cultural Center. The exhibit, titled *Reconfigurations: Art, Disability, Identity*, also included the work of eleven-year-old Aedan Ptak, who has Down syndrome, along with that of Aedan's dad, Anthony.

Given your own experiences, how would you have written about the differences between illness and disability? Although some medical professionals might call Down syndrome a disease, your life and writing were more nuanced about the distinctions. Certainly the two often overlap, since many disabilities are accompanied by disease, and many diseases are disabling. But when you wrote as the mother of a child with Down syndrome and as someone with a brain tumor, you offered crucial perspective on why we should not collapse the two categories. Disease is, by definition, an unwanted, pathological state, whereas disabilities are more ambiguous. And where disease is associated with suffering, limitation, and pathology, disability is not necessarily so. Granted, some people with disabilities wish to be able-bodied, but many—particularly those living with conditions such as deafness, autism, dwarfism, and Down syndrome—say they are perfectly happy as they are. While they may want the world to be more accommodating, they do not want their bodies or minds to be different. Anyone seeing the vibrant young ASL (American Sign Language) poets featured in the documentary *Deaf Jam* or the rich and satisfying family life of Joe Stramondo and Leah Smith, who have achondroplasia and star in *Far from the Tree*, would recognize that some disabilities coexist with health and well-being.

Writing about Maybelle, you were at your most joyful, compelling, and open-minded. You were passionate about your beliefs but were also attuned to the possibility that your convictions would evolve with time. One of your most important political statements came from writing honestly about previous abortions, which you held up in contrast to your wanted pregnancy with Maybelle. It is hard to imagine a better case for experience as a basis to defend reproductive rights. For you, those freedoms included not only access to safe and legal abortions but also support to continue a wanted pregnancy after a prenatal diagnosis. You wrote about your commitment to Maybelle's inclusion in education and social life, your determination to teach her how to ride a bike, and the joys of being her parent. One of my favorite passages in this book describes the pleasures of dancing with Maybelle in the morning before school. I remember you telling me about the two of you eating cereal for dinner on the couch in front of the TV. To hell with perfect mommies who serve perfect meals to families gathered around the table! You emphasized the importance of shaping routines and rituals around families' own beliefs and values rather than social conventions. As Maybelle grew from a baby to a child, your thinking evolved from minimizing her differences from typical children to embracing them as part of what made her unique and valued.

You wrote about your illness with similar honesty and insight. But while you never hesitated to fight for social justice, you did not imagine disease in terms of fighting. You avoided the kind of bellicose language criticized by Susan Sontag in *Illness as Metaphor*.[24] While some are energized by speaking about cancer in terms of declarations of war, battle, opposition, and overcoming, such language problematically divides the ill into winners and losers, implying that those who succumb to disease just didn't fight hard enough. It also puts the ill person into a constant state of embattlement with her own body, ensuring that the end of life will be dominated by conflict rather than acceptance.

You certainly didn't welcome your tumor. But you wrote of living with it, imagining it, owning it, terms that acknowledge illness as a part of your body-mind rather than an invading enemy. At the same time, you described your grief and fear on learning that your tumor was growing, especially your worry that the cancer would limit your time with Maybelle. Whereas you saw disability in terms of opportunity to affirm and welcome difference, disease was responsible for the devastating loss of independence, ability, and dignity. "I am a tenured full professor who can't pee without help," you wrote in your final, wrenching goodbye column.[25] Throughout your illness, you also acknowledged sickness and death as a part of life and gave us a model of a good death. In *Being Mortal*—a book whose wisdom you cherished—Atul Gawande writes that aggressive metaphors for cancer encourage patients to endure grueling treatments after all hope for survival is gone. For loved ones, the experience of witnessing such terrible suffering can prolong the trauma and grief of death. By contrast, your dying process allowed time for reflection on Gawande's end-of-life questions:

1. What is your understanding of where you are and of your illness?
2. Your fears or worries for the future
3. Your goals and priorities
4. What outcomes are unacceptable to you? What are you willing to sacrifice and not?

And later,

5. What would a good day look like?[26]

Alison, I'm thankful that there was time for goodbyes. Mine involved learning to knit socks and sending my first lumpy pair to the wrong address. When they eventually arrived at your home, you sent me a gracious thank you with a picture of your stocking feet. There was time to eat the cinnamon rolls you loved and throw a princess party for Maybelle. You died with your beloved partner, Brian, at your side. There is only space here for me to consider briefly the profound messages about illness communicated by the way you lived and died. Had you lived on, I'm sure you would have translated your experiences into reflection on the ethical and political implications of distinguishing disability from disease.

How special is Down syndrome in this book? How much do your conclusions apply exclusively to Down syndrome, and how much do they represent people with intellectual disabilities, or disability more generally? Advocating for disability justice is challenging because disability is such a diverse category, encompassing a wide spectrum of bodyminds that sometimes have competing agendas. To what extent is any one person or group representative of a broader disability contingent? And to what extent do the insights you offer in this book apply beyond the particular example of Down syndrome? In a more perfect world, I would challenge you to answer these questions as you revised the manuscript.

On the one hand, you might say, Down syndrome is unique. It is the most common and best known of all genetic disabilities. It has a history of its own that might begin with the appearance of people with Down syndrome in works of art and literature. There are the ancient sculptures of people with features suggesting Down syndrome found by archaeologists in Egypt and Mexico; the painting *Adoration of the Christ Child*, by Jan Joest van Kalkar in 1515; and William Faulkner's modernist classic *The Sound and the Fury*. Or its unique history might have a more medical slant, starting with the syndrome named by John Langdon Down, a nineteenth-century physician, or with Jerome Lejeune's discovery of trisomy 21, the chromosomal anomaly that gives rise to Down syndrome, in the early 1950s. The history would include the development of amniocentesis, the increasingly routine use of prenatal testing, and the rise of a lucrative industry represented by companies like MaterniT21 and Sequenom. It would also include the founding of advocacy organizations like the National Down Syndrome Society in 1979 and the National Down Syndrome Congress in 1973. And its heroes would include activists like Emily and Jason Kingsley, actors Chris Burke and Pablo Pineda, athletes Jonathan Stocklosa and Karen Gaffney, artist Judith Scott, and model Madeline Stuart.

On the other hand, Down syndrome is representative of a broader disability experience. Once medically defined as "Mongoloid idiots," people with Down syndrome have suffered the same history of discrimination, institutionalization, poor health care, and low expectations that so many other groups marked by physical and intellectual disabilities have had to endure. Like other people with disabilities, people with Down syndrome were subject to death by exposure, buried in unmarked graves, and sent to the Nazi gas chambers. Less sensationally, their lives were generally foreshortened, and their abilities thwarted, by inadequate education and medical care. And like other people with disabilities, many people with Down syndrome are thriving now that they are commonly raised by their own families and have access to regular health care, school, and work. They still face many of the same challenges of prejudice, low expectations, and lack of opportunities that other people with disabilities encounter. They also have the same needs and desires: to be included in education, family, and social life; to enjoy opportunities for meaningful education, work, health care, and social experiences; and to have accommodations to maximize their autonomy and well-being.

I'm fairly confident your answer would go along these lines: Down syndrome is both representative and unique, as are Maybelle and other individuals with the condition. This means that the book you have written will contribute not only to the community of people with Down syndrome and their supporters but also to people with all sorts of disabilities, particularly the disabilities that include both intellectual and physical differences. But the book also offers more universal insights that go beyond the special and the inclusive. It shows how love and grief, loss and opportunity, can go hand in hand; how difference can bring creativity and change; how mortality makes time meaningful and precious.

In the spirit of collaboration and dialogue that constitutes the production of this book and so much of your work, I give you the last word. I think you would have described this as a feminist book, in keeping with the definition of feminism you once offered in an interview: "a social and theoretical movement that works to eradicate all forms of oppression that keep people from achieving their full humanity."[27]

ACKNOWLEDGMENTS

Our first thanks go to Alison herself, for the gift of trusting us with this project. Alison's unfinished manuscript represented years of dedicated research and writing, work she threaded between the daily tasks of parenthood, teaching, and activism, all the while coping with the effects of both cancer and its treatment. To know all this was daunting, as was completing a work that was true to Alison's vision and worthy of her standards. Because we took on the project late in Alison's illness, we could not discuss with her the book's substance and scope in detail. But by email and FaceTime, she conveyed her trust in us; we have done our best to complete a book worthy of that trust and of our shared friendship.

Throughout our collaboration, we—George and Rachel—developed a deep and lasting appreciation for each other. We feel as if Alison understood that this project would be a way not only to honor and continue our connection with her but also to solidify the mutual respect and friendship between us, her co-authors. It has been a comfort and a joy to work together to bring Alison's accomplishments into the world.

Alison's husband, Brian McGee, has been unfailingly helpful in an extraordinarily difficult time, providing Alison's drafts and notes on this project, answering inquiries, and affirming our work. We are grateful for his friendship, guidance, and support. Alison's dear friends Catherine Bush and Cindi May have also provided invaluable guidance, for which we are grateful. Thanks to our friend Jordana Mendelson; to Alison's many interview subjects, especially Emily Perl Kingsley, Stephanie Meredith, Bridget Brown, Nancy Brown, Meriah Hudson, and Kathryn Lang. And though Alison's many friendships and connections with colleagues make a comprehensive list impossible, we know she would have liked us to thank her writing group, the Super Ninja Writing Force: Claire Curtis and the late Conseula Francis. "It has been absolutely essential to my professional life," Alison wrote in an email to George. "I would never have finished an article or chapter without that writing group."

We would also like to thank Ilene Kalish and her team at New York University Press for overseeing this project from proposal to manuscript to book. Special thanks go to Anna Krauthamer, for her help preparing the manuscript for publication, and to copyeditor Patricia Boyd, for her thorough reading and thoughtful suggestions.

While Alison was with us, three panels (the American Studies Association conference in Atlanta, GiGi's Playhouse Down Syndrome Achievement Center in New York City, and Columbia University [with generous sponsorship from the university's Heyman Center for the Humanities]), helped us collaborate and cement our friendship.

Finally, we acknowledge Alison's family: her parents, Lee and Kelly Piepmeier; her brother, Trey Piepmeier, and his partner, Olivia Miller; her brother, Aaron Piepmeier, Aaron's wife, Mary Piepmeier, and their daughter, Margot; and Alison's daughter, Maybelle Biffle-Piepmeier, to whom this book is dedicated.

INDIVIDUAL ACKNOWLEDGMENTS

In September 2017, George presented an early version of chapter 5 at Vanderbilt University, Alison's alma mater, as the Alison Piepmeier Memorial Lecture. He is grateful to Rory Dicker and Mona Frederick at Vanderbilt for the invitation. He also thanks Sarah Mesle and Sarah Blackwood at *Avidly* for publishing his essay "For Alison." And as always, he thanks his wife, Theresa Filtz, and his daughters, Ellie Estreich and Laura Estreich, for their support.

Rachel expresses personal thanks to Rob Spirko, who first suggested that she should know his friend Alison Piepmeier; to Tom Lutz at *Los Angeles Review of Books* for publishing her essay "Blogging Illness"; to Emily Perl Kingsley for the steadfast support she has shown to Alison, Rachel, and their generation of mothers; to Jon and Noah, for their forbearance; and to her son, Henry, for making possible the wonderful network of connections underlying this project.

NOTES

PREFACE

1 Brian McGee, "Guest Blog: Alison's Time," *Every Little Thing* (blog), August 17, 2016, https://alisonpiepmeier.blogspot.com.

2 Alison Kafer, *Feminist, Queer, Crip* (Bloomington: Indiana University Press, 2013); Ellen Samuels, "Six Ways of Looking at Crip Time," *Disability Studies Quarterly* 37, no. 3 (August 2017), http://dx.doi.org; Robert McRuer, *Crip Times: Disability, Globalization, and Resistance* (New York: New York University Press, 2018).

3 Elaine Scarry, *The Body in Pain: The Making and Unmaking of the World* (New York: Oxford University Press, 1987).

4 For example, see Michael Bérubé, *The Secret Life of Stories: From Don Quixote to Harry Potter, How Understanding Intellectual Disability Transforms the Way We Read* (New York: New York University Press, 2016).

5 Rita Charon, *Narrative Medicine: Honoring the Stories of Illness* (New York: Oxford University Press, 2006); Rita Charon et al., *The Principles and Practice of Narrative Medicine* (New York: Oxford University Press, 2016); Rita Charon, ed., *Stories Matter: The Role of Narrative in Medical Ethics* (New York: Routledge, 2002).

6 Amy Shuman, *Other People's Stories: Entitlement Claims and the Critique of Empathy* (Urbana: University of Illinois Press, 2010).

7 Lee Edelman, *No Future: Queer Theory and the Death Drive* (Durham, NC: Duke University Press, 2004); Jack Halberstam, *The Queer Art of Failure* (Durham, NC: Duke University Press, 2014); José Esteban Muñoz, *Cruising Utopia: The Then and There of Queer Futurity* (New York: New York University Press, 2009); Kathryn Bond Stockton, *The Queer Child, or Growing Sideways in the Twentieth Century* (Durham, NC: Duke University Press, 2009).

8 Eudora Welty, "The Making of a Writer: Listening in the Dark," *New York Times*, October 9, 1983, https://archive.nytimes.com.

9 Alison Piepmeier, "Princess Leia Taught Me to Be Tough," *Charleston City Paper*, May 27, 2015, www.charlestoncitypaper.com.

10 Alison Piepmeier, "What a Shattered Coffee Cup Says about Life," *Charleston City Paper*, June 2, 2016, www.charlestoncitypaper.com.

11 Alison Piepmeier, "A Beautifully Mended Princess Leia," *Every Little Thing* (blog), June 26, 2016, http://alisonpiepmeier.blogspot.com.

1. "I WOULDN'T CHANGE YOU IF I COULD"

1 Barbara Katz Rothman, *The Tentative Pregnancy: How Amniocentesis Changes the Experience of Motherhood* (New York: W.W. Norton & Company, 1993), 87.

2 Landsman, *Reconstructing Motherhood*, 9.

3 Simi Linton, *Claiming Disability: Knowledge and Identity* (New York: New York University Press, 1998), 11.

4 Linton, *Claiming Disability*, 8–17.

5 Landsman, *Reconstructing Motherhood*, 173.

6 Emily Perl Kingsley, "Welcome to Holland," 1987, www.ndss.org.

7 Bérubé, *Life as We Know It*, 26.

2. THE INADEQUACY OF "CHOICE"

1 Alison Piepmeier, "Choosing to Have a Child with Down Syndrome," *Motherlode* (blog), *New York Times*, March 2, 2012, parenting.blogs.nytimes.com.

2 Various authors, comments on Alison Piepmeier, "Choosing to Have a Child with Down Syndrome," *Motherlode* (blog), *New York Times*, March 2, 2012, parenting. blogs.nytimes.com.

3 Joan Rothschild, *The Dream of the Perfect Child* (Bloomington: Indiana University Press, 2005), 146–148, 175–176.

4 Marsha Saxton, "Born and Unborn: The Implications of Reproductive Technologies for People with Disabilities," in *Test-Tube Women: What Future for Motherhood?*, ed. Rita Arditti, Renate Duelli Klein, and Shelley Minden (London: Pandora Press, 1984), 302. Italics in original.

5 Marsha Saxton, "Disability Rights and Selective Abortion," in *Abortion Wars: A Half Century of Struggle, 1950–2000*, ed. Rickie Solinger (Berkeley: University of California Press, 1998), 375, 389. Italics in original.

6 Karen Bender and Nina de Gramont, *Choice: True Stories of Birth, Contraception, Infertility, Adoption, Single Parenthood and Abortion* (New York: MacAdam/Cage, 2007), 12.

7 In the fall of 2011, a maternal blood test that was introduced offered genetic information about the fetus in the first trimester of pregnancy, without a risk of miscarriage. Since then, the number of available tests, and the market for them, has expanded dramatically.

8 One of the most important studies of prenatal testing, Erik Parens and Adrienne Asch, *Prenatal Testing and Disability Rights* (Washington, DC: Georgetown University Press, 2000), contains a number of feminist explorations of selective abortion and was published before Wolf's and Richards's books.

9 Naomi Wolf, *Misconceptions: Truth, Lies, and the Unexpected on the Journey to Motherhood* (New York: Anchor, 2001), 40. The AFP (alpha-fetoprotein) test uses

maternal blood to screen for neural tube conditions and chromosomal conditions, including spina bifida and Down syndrome.

10 Amy Richards, *Opting In: Having a Child without Losing Yourself* (New York: Farrar, Straus, and Giroux, 2008), 112.

11 For examples of information that potential parents are given during prenatal testing, see Brian G. Skotko, Susan P. Levine, and Richard Goldstein, "Having a Son or Daughter with Down Syndrome: Perspectives from Mothers and Fathers," *American Journal of Medical Genetics* part A 155, no. 10 (October 2011): 2335–2347; Brian G. Skotko, Priya S. Kishnani, and George T. Capone (Down Syndrome Diagnosis Study Group), "Prenatal Diagnosis of Down Syndrome: How Best to Deliver the News," *American Journal of Medical Genetics* part A 149A, no. 11 (November 2009): 2361–2367. One woman I interviewed said that her older child's pediatrician told her that children with Down syndrome are routinely institutionalized. That has not been true for forty years, and yet she based her decision to terminate partly on shockingly inaccurate information from a medical professional.

12 Rothman, *Tentative Pregnancy*, 180, 187.

13 Rothman, *Tentative Pregnancy*, 61, 75, 76.

14 Dena S. Davis, *Genetic Dilemmas: Reproductive Technology, Parental Choices, and Children's Futures* (New York: Oxford University Press, 2009), 17.

15 Davis, *Genetic Dilemmas*, 19.

16 Davis, *Genetic Dilemmas*, 84.

17 Davis, *Genetic Dilemmas*, 84–85.

18 Rosemarie Garland-Thomson, "Integrating Disability, Transforming Feminist Theory," *NWSA Journal* 14, no. 3 (2002): 5.

19 Ginsburg and Rapp, "Enabling Disability," 189.

20 These interviews amounted to 287,433 words of transcribed data.

21 College of Charleston Institutional Review Board approval code GJJQ-05-02-2011.

22 I identified some women of color through online communities of bloggers who are parents of children with Down syndrome. Others came to me via a graduate student, Michael Owens, who spent two semesters doing independent studies of people of color who are parents of children with disabilities. He told the parents about my research, and several were willing to talk with me. All the women of color with whom I spoke said that the other parents of children with Down syndrome with whom they interact are white.

23 As Sujatha Jesudason and Julia Epstein note, "feminist disability advocates end up feeling shut out of reproductive rights conversations because they assume their pro-choice counterparts believe any questioning of pregnancy termination to be anti-choice." Sujatha Jesudason and Julia Epstein, "The Paradox of Disability in Abortion Debates: Bringing the Pro-Choice and Disability Rights Communities Together," *Contraception* 84, no. 6 (2011): 541–543, www.contraceptionjournal.org. Kafer, *Feminist, Queer, Crip*, 163, makes a similar observation.

24 Some names of the people I interviewed have been changed, because of their preferences. The names of all the children have been changed.

25 Jael Silliman, Marlene Gerber Fried, Loretta Ross, and Elena R. Gutierrez, *Undivided Rights: Women of Color Organize for Reproductive Justice* (Cambridge, MA: South End Press, 2004), 4.

26 Kafer, *Feminist, Queer, Crip*, 162.

27 I align my political views with those of Kafer, *Feminist, Queer, Crip*, 167: "Abortion for any reason and under any circumstance must then be accompanied by accessible and affordable prenatal care for all women, as well as reliable and affordable child care, access to social services, and the kind of information about and supports for disability mandated in the Kennedy Brownback Act."

28 Dorothy Roberts, *Killing the Black Body: Race, Reproduction, and the Meaning of Liberty* (New York: Pantheon Books, 1997), 6. Italics in original. The term *reproductive justice* emerged after Roberts's book was published, so she uses the terms *reproductive liberty* and *reproductive freedom*.

29 Rothman, *Tentative Pregnancy*, 189.

30 For instance, well-respected abortion scholar Rickie Solinger argues, "I am convinced that choice is a remarkably unstable, undependable foundation for guaranteeing women's control over their own bodies, their reproductive lives, their motherhood, and ultimately their status as full citizens." Rickie Solinger, *Beggars and Choosers: How the Politics of Choice Shapes Adoption, Abortion, and Welfare in the United States* (New York: Hill and Wang, 2001), 7. In January 2013, Planned Parenthood gave up the *pro-choice* label to characterize its work. Andrea Smith criticizes the "pro-life versus pro-choice advocates who make their overall political goal either the criminalization or decriminalization of abortion," noting that reproduction depends not only on individuals but also on communities. Andrea Smith, "Beyond Pro-Choice Versus Pro-Life: Women of Color and Reproductive Justice," *NWSA Journal* 17, no. 1 (2005): 120. Dorothy Roberts and Sujatha Jesudason, "Movement Intersectionality: The Case of Race, Gender, Disability, and Genetic Technologies," *Du Bois Review: Social Science Research on Race* 10, no. 2 (2014): 313–328, doi:10.1017/S1742058X13000210, argue that advocates must "recognize the relationship of individual lives to larger social, political, and economic factors, and the intersectional and contextual nature of individual and family decision making. They appreciate that the difficult decisions that women and people with disabilities make must be understood in terms of structural and pervasive inequality, mistreatment, and bias."

31 Kafer, *Feminist, Queer, Crip*, 162.

32 Adrienne Asch and David Wasserman, "Where Is the Sin in Synecdoche? Prenatal Testing and the Parent-Child Relationship," in *Quality of Life and Human Difference: Genetic Testing, Health Care, and Disability*, ed. David Wasserman,

Jerome Bickenbach, and Robert Wachbroit (New York: Cambridge University Press, 2005), 182, 174.

33 Kimala Price, "What Is Reproductive Justice? How Women of Color Activists Are Redefining the Pro-Choice Paradigm," *Meridians: Feminism, Race, Transnationalism* 10, no. 2 (2010): 43.

34 Generations Ahead, *Bridging the Divide*, 116.

35 "Our bodies need care; we need assistance to live; we are fragile, limited, and pliable in the face of life itself. Disability is thus inherent in our being: What we call disability is perhaps the essential characteristic of being human." Rosemarie Garland-Thomson, "The Case for Conserving Disability," *Bioethical Inquiry* 9, no. 3 (September 2012): 342.

36 Silliman et al., *Undivided Rights*, 4.

3. THE WELCOME TABLE

1 Harriet McBryde Johnson, "Unspeakable Conversations," *New York Times Magazine*, February 16, 2003, www.nytimes.com.

2 Johnson, *Too Late to Die Young*, 221.

3 Johnson, *Too Late to Die Young*, 223.

4 Peter Singer, "Happy Nevertheless," *New York Times Magazine*, December 24, 2008, www.nytimes.com.

5 Bérubé, *Life as We Know It*, 264.

4. SAINTS, SAGES, AND VICTIMS

1 Groneberg, *Road Map to Holland*, 84.

2 Groneberg, *Road Map to Holland*, 159–160.

3 Groneberg, *Road Map to Holland*, 212–213.

4 Autobiography scholar G. Thomas Couser, *Signifying Bodies*, 3, notes, "Although it is often not recognized as such, eluding most critics' radar, disability has become one of the pervasive topics of contemporary life writing."

5 For instance, Bernstein, *Rachel in the World*, received glowing reviews from *Kirkus Reviews*, *Booklist*, and *Library Journal*. Collins, *Not Even Wrong*, received positive reviews from major newspapers and *Vanity Fair* and *Entertainment Weekly*. Several of these memoirs have been award-winners: Bérubé, *Life As We Know It*, was a *New York Times* Notable Book of the Year, and Kephart, *A Slant of Sun*, was a National Book Award finalist. Forman, *This Lovely Life*, was named winner of the PEN Center Literary Award in Creative Nonfiction and the Bread Loaf Writers Conference Bakeless Prize in Creative Nonfiction and was chosen as one of the best one hundred books of 2009 by the *San Francisco Chronicle*.

6 Couser examines the larger trend in *Signifying Bodies*, and other scholars, such as Susannah Mintz, examine other cohorts writing such memoirs (Mintz, for instance, examines authors who have disabilities as well as sibling narratives in

Unruly Bodies). No one, however, has examined the parent memoir as a genre. In a book review essay, Bruce Mills, "Nothing about Us, without Us" (review of *Weather Reports from the Autism Front: A Father's Memoir of His Autistic Son*, by James C. Wilson, and *The Only Boy in the World: A Father Explores the Mysteries of Autism*, by Michael Blastland), *Disability Studies Quarterly* 30, no. 1 (2010), www.dsq-sds.org, offers a brief and compelling analysis of two memoirs by parents of children with autism.

7 It seems that the challenge of writing about disability is specific to book-length parenting memoirs. I haven't noticed the same tendencies in collections of parent essays, such as Yantra Bertelli, Jennifer Silverman, and Sarah Talbot, eds., *My Baby Rides the Short Bus: The Unabashedly Human Experience of Raising Kids with Disabilities* (Oakland, CA: PM Press, 2009), or in all blogs by parents of kids with disabilities. Savarese and Savarese, "'The Superior Half of Speaking,'" however, note that "parent bloggers and autism organizations" do "perseverate on the difficulties" of raising a child with autism.

8 Couser, *Signifying Bodies*, 6–7.

9 Mintz, *Unruly Bodies*, 22.

10 Couser, *Vulnerable Subjects*, 68.

11 Couser *Signifying Bodies*, 6–7, notes that disability memoirs have an activist tendency: "What links these books is the fundamental endeavor to destigmatize various anomalous bodily conditions. Disability memoir should be seen, therefore, not as spontaneous self-expression but as a response—indeed a retort—to the traditional misrepresentation of disability in Western culture generally." More specifically discussing parental memoirs, Couser, *Vulnerable Subjects*, 69, says, "In most [parental narratives of disabled children], political and parental functions are one: the narrator's role as advocate for children with disabilities is an extension of his or her role as parent." Similarly, Mintz, *Unruly Bodies*, 22, notes, "Autobiography might reinvent disability, for readers as much as writers, in dramatically liberatory ways." But this isn't what happens in most parent memoirs, and despite Couser's optimism about these memoirs, he too expresses concern about the political effects of a parental memoir that "describes people like you as not quite human and that is devoted explicitly to preventing the future (re)production of people like yourself" (Couser, *Vulnerable Subjects*, 68). Interestingly, he offers no examples of the parental memoirs that demonstrate advocacy.

12 Bérubé, *Life as We Know It*, 255, articulates the importance of cultural narratives: "Part of the burden of representation, for human populations that have long been 'dehumanized,' is precisely to demonstrate that 'dehumanized' people do in fact *have* feelings and dreams just as you do."

13 Allison Carey, *On the Margins of Citizenship: Intellectual Disability and Civil Rights in Twentieth-Century America* (Philadelphia: Temple University Press, 2007), especially chapter 6.

14 Bérubé, *Life as We Know It*, 27.

15 Couser, *Signifying Bodies*, 6–7.

16 Ginsburg and Rapp, "Enabling Disability," 181; Janice McLaughlin, Dan Goodley, Emma Clavering, and Pamela Fisher, *Families Raising Disabled Children: Enabling Care and Social Justice* (London: Palgrave Macmillan, 2008), 60, similarly describe them as "sense making."

17 Dale Evans, *Angel Unaware* (Grand Rapids: Revell, 1953).

18 Twelve of the nineteen monographs I've read have been published since 2000: Bernstein, *Rachel in the World* (2007); Collins, *Not Even Wrong* (2004); Forman, *This Lovely Life* (2009); Fournier, *Where We Going, Daddy?* (2008); Richard Galli, *Rescuing Jeffrey* (Chapel Hill, NC: Algonquin Books of Chapel Hill, 2000); Groneberg, *Road Map to Holland* (2008); Mont, *Different Kind of Boy* (2002); Moore, *George & Sam* (2004); Park, *Exiting Nirvana* (2001); Rummel-Hudson, *Schuyler's Monster* (2008); Savarese, *Reasonable People* (2007); and Soper, *The Year My Son and I Were Born* (2009). Of the additional six, three were published since 1995: Martha Beck, *Expecting Adam: A True Story of Birth, Rebirth, and Everyday Magic* (New York: Times Books, 1999); Bérubé, *Life as We Know It* (1996); and Kephart, *A Slant of Sun* (1998). Only five were published before 1995 and function as texts that helped establish the genre: Bernstein, *Loving Rachel* (1988), Evans, *Angel Unaware* (1953); Martha Moraghan Jablow, *Cara: Growing with a Retarded Child* (Philadelphia: Temple University Press, 1982); Fern Kupfer, *Before and After Zachariah: A True Story about a Family and a Different Kind of Courage* (Chicago: Academy Chicago, 1988); and Park, *The Siege* (1967). All but two of these texts were written by parents in the United States; Fournier, *Where We Going, Daddy?*, is French, and Moore, *George & Sam*, is British.

19 Nine of the nineteen memoirs were written by academics. The fact that all the memoirists in this study are white and middle-class suggests nothing about the distribution of disabilities throughout a population but instead suggests that certain parents have the idea, the inclination, and the support to write a memoir while raising a child.

20 Bernstein, *Loving Rachel*, 47.

21 Soper, *Year My Son and I Were Born*, 131.

22 Kephart, *Slant of Sun*, 77.

23 Kephart, *Slant of Sun*, 149.

24 A. Jupin, "Beautifully Written; an Honest Look into an Extraordinary Experience," customer review of *Road Map to Holland*, by Groneberg, Amazon.com, June 7, 2008, www.amazon.com.

25 Not all parents who read such books value the grieving tone, however. One mother interviewed by McLaughlin and colleagues said of a memoir she had read, "I got this book after I had Luke, I was pleased I didn't get this when I was pregnant; it was the story of this girl and this mum and it was all how the mum

felt, how she felt sorry for herself and it was about the girl growing up and how the mam found it difficult and, I found it a very selfish book." McLaughlin et al., *Families Raising Disabled Children*, 171.

26 Bernstein, *Rachel in the World*, 6, 7.

27 McLaughlin et al., *Families Raising Disabled Children*, 14, note that recent research has demonstrated that, in terms of "psychological trauma and suicidal thoughts . . . no actual difference existed between parents of disabled and non-disabled children." Indeed, there is now evidence that having a child with a disability adds life skills to parents and siblings.

28 Forman, *This Lovely Life*, 156.

29 Forman, *This Lovely Life*, 156–157.

30 Fournier, *Where We Going, Daddy?*, 31.

31 Fournier, *Where We Going, Daddy?*, 1.

32 Cord Jefferson, review of *Where We Going, Daddy?*, by Fournier, *NPR*, August 18, 2010, www.npr.org. For the excerpt of Fournier, *Where We Going, Daddy?*, see Jean-Louis Fournier, "Excerpt: 'Where We Going, Daddy?,'" *NPR*, August 17, 2020, www.npr.org. Other memoirs have received similar acclaim.

33 Linton, *Claiming Disability*, 162.

34 Forman, *This Lovely Life*, 94.

35 For example, Kupfer, *Before and After Zachariah*; Kephart, *Slant of Sun*; Forman, *This Lovely Life*; Rummel-Hudson, *Schuyler's Monster*; and Bernstein, *Loving Rachel*, all document this extended process of trying to pin down the child's diagnosis.

36 Bérubé, *Life As We Know It*, 76, notes, "I suspect that there may be *something* wrong about a sociomedical apparatus that devotes so much of its resources to identifying Down syndrome in utero, instead of devoting resources to finding out how to treat Down syndrome symptomatically ex utero."

37 Lennard Davis, *Bending Over Backwards: Essays on Disability and the Body* (New York: New York University Press, 2002), 237.

38 Fournier, *Where We Going, Daddy?*, 20.

39 Fournier, *Where We Going, Daddy?*, 21.

40 Fournier, *Where We Going, Daddy?*, 22.

41 Fournier, *Where We Going, Daddy?*, 41.

42 Park, *Exiting Nirvana*, 32.

43 Park, *Exiting Nirvana*, 33.

44 Park, *Exiting Nirvana*, 171.

45 Bernstein, *Loving Rachel*, 49.

46 Forman, *This Lovely Life*, 188.

47 For instance, national Down syndrome organizations, including the National Down Syndrome Society (www.ndss.org) and the National Down Syndrome Congress (www.ndsc.org), have targeted the term *retarded*. The Associated Press

stopped using the term in 2008, and in 2010 legislation was approved that removed the term from all federal documents, replacing it with *intellectual disability*.

48 Collins, *Not Even Wrong*, 85.

49 Moore, *George & Sam*, 210, 279, compares autism and Down syndrome as well, although she seems to argue that Down syndrome is easier on the family than autism is.

50 In 1994, philosopher Peter Singer wrote, "To have a child with Down syndrome is to have a very different experience from having a normal child. It can still be a warm and loving experience, but we must have lowered expectations of our child's ability. We cannot expect a child with Down syndrome to play the guitar, to develop an appreciation of science fiction, to learn a foreign language, to chat with us about the latest Woody Allen movie, or to be a respectable athlete, basketballer or tennis player." Singer, *Rethinking Life and Death* (New York: St. Martin's Griffin, 1996), 213. Bérubé, "Equality, Freedom, and/or Justice for All," 107, describes an exchange between himself and Singer. In their discussion, Bérubé clearly (and with more kindness than I might muster) articulates that the cultural understanding of what "we cannot expect" for people with Down syndrome or other cognitive disabilities is fairly arbitrary but has significant repercussions. In her memoir, Harriet McBryde Johnson recounts a similar encounter with Singer, who made the argument that people with significant physical disabilities lack the ability to enjoy pleasures such as visiting the beach—despite Johnson's own stories about playing on the beach as a child. Even basic factual information can be completely missed when people believe the stereotypes. As Johnson, *Too Late to Die Young*, 54, explains, "When bigotry is the dominant view, it sounds like self-evident truth."

51 McLaughlin et al., *Families Raising Disabled Children*, 15.

52 As Rosemarie Garland-Thomson, *Staring: How We Look* (New York: Oxford University Press, 2009), 19, explains, "Each one of us ineluctably acquires one or more disabilities—naming them variably as illness, disease, injury, old age, failure, dysfunction, or dependence. This inconvenient truth nudges most of us who think of ourselves as able-bodied toward imagining disability as an uncommon visitation that mostly happens to someone else, as a fate somehow elective rather than inevitable. In response, we have refused to see disability."

53 Eva Feder Kittay, ed., *Cognitive Disability and Its Challenge to Moral Philosophy* (New York: Wiley-Blackwell, 2010), 406–407.

54 Savarese, *Reasonable People*, xiv.

55 Savarese, *Reasonable People*, xxix.

56 Collins, *Not Even Wrong*, 85.

57 Soper, *Year My Son and I Were Born*, 296.

58 Soper, *Year My Son and I Were Born*, 303.

59 Johnson, *Too Late to Die Young*, 253.

60 Kittay, "When Caring Is Just," 567.

61 Bérubé, *Life As We Know It*, 125.

62 Bérubé, *Life As We Know It*, 127.

63 Bérubé, *Life As We Know It*, 128.

64 "Every step would be prolonged and arduous, every triumph precious and magnified." Bérubé, *Life As We Know It*, 131.

65 Savarese, *Reasonable People*, 265.

66 Kephart, *Slant of Sun*, 239.

67 Forman, *This Lovely Life*, 233.

68 Groneberg, *Road Map to Holland*, 222.

69 Moore, *George & Sam*, 275.

70 McLaughlin et al., *Families Raising Disabled Children*, 15.

71 Bérubé, *Life As We Know It*, 176.

72 Kittay is widely recognized for her important work articulating dependence as a foundational human characteristic, especially in Kittay, *Love's Labour*.

73 Savarese, *Reasonable People*, 286.

74 Kephart, *Slant of Sun*, 232. Anthropologist Gail Heidi Landsman has found a similar political phenomenon among mothers of children with disabilities: "A number of mothers in the study describe a personal transformation in terms not only of rejecting the binary of normal/abnormal, but of embracing the very qualities in their child that are labeled by society as abnormal. The child's impairment is in this interpretation not relegated exclusively to a biology separate from the self, but rather is understood as integral to the child and infused with meaning." Landsman, *Reconstructing Motherhood*, 207.

75 Park, *Exiting Nirvana*, 24. Interestingly, even as Park herself resists this narrative, a review written by Megan Rutherford of *Time* magazine and printed on the back of Park's book proclaims "her [Jessy's] story is nonetheless one of triumph." The formulaic narratives die hard.

76 Savarese, *Reasonable People*, 429.

77 Ginsburg and Rapp, "Enabling Disability," 189.

78 Landsman, *Reconstructing Motherhood*, 173, suggests that "what mothers of disabled children have come to know can be used to further our understanding of humanity and to promote the expression and experience of full lives for all people."

5. ACCESSIBLE WORDS

1 Bess Williamson, "Access," in *Keywords for Disability Studies*, ed. Rachel Adams, Benjamin Reiss, and David Serlin (New York: New York University Press, 2015), 14.

2 Joseph P. Shapiro, *No Pity: People with Disabilities Forging a New Civil Rights Movement* (New York: Random House, 1994), 3.

3   Phillip Lopate, introduction to *The Art of the Personal Essay*, ed. Phillip Lopate (New York: Random House, 1994), xxiv.

4   Alison Piepmeier, "Feminist Disability Studies Scholar Attends the NSGC," *Every Little Thing* (blog), October 10, 2013, http://alisonpiepmeier.blogspot.com.

5   Alison Piepmeier, "Waffles," *Every Little Thing* (blog), May 5, 2013, https://alisonpiepmeier.blogspot.com.

6   Alison Piepmeier, "Important Life Truths," *Every Little Thing* (blog), November 13, 2013, https://alisonpiepmeier.blogspot.com.

7   Kenkō, *Essays in Idleness*, trans. Donald Keene (New York: Columbia University Press, 1998), 134.

8   Alison Piepmeier, "No Fashion Sense," *Every Little Thing* (blog), February 15, 2013, https://alisonpiepmeier.blogspot.com.

9   G. Thomas Couser, "Illness," in *Keywords for Disability Studies*, ed. Rachel Adams, Benjamin Reiss, and David Serlin (New York: New York University Press, 2015), 105.

10 Alison Piepmeier, "The Writing Process," *Every Little Thing* (blog), June 18, 2014, https://alisonpiepmeier.blogspot.com.

11 Alison Piepmeier, "Exploring My Own Disability. And My Own Ego," *Every Little Thing* (blog), March 20, 2014, https://alisonpiepmeier.blogspot.com.

6. SIX QUESTIONS ON THE SPECIAL, THE INCLUSIVE, AND THE UNIVERSAL

1   See, for example, "Which Direct-to-Consumer Genetic Test to Choose?," *The Medical Futurist*, March 20, 2018, https://medicalfuturist.com.

2   David Reich, "How Genetics Is Changing Our Understanding of 'Race,'" *New York Times*, March 23, 2018, www.nytimes.com. For a response, see "How Not to Talk about Race and Genetics," *Buzzfeed* Opinion, March 30, 2018, www.buzzfeednews.com.

3   Ruth Padawer, "Sigrid Johnson Was Black. A DNA Test Said She Wasn't." *New York Times*, November 19, 2018, www.nytimes.com.

4   Progenity home page, www.progenity.com.

5   On the applications and dangers of CRISPR, see, for example, Mazhar Adli, Prashant Mali, Stanley L. Qi, and David R. Liu, eds., "CRISPR: From the Basic Biology to Its Technological Applications," *Journal of Molecular Biology*, 431, no. 1 (January 2019): 1–122; Jennifer Doudna and Emmanuel Charpentier, "The New Frontier of Genome Engineering with CRISPR-Cas 9," *Science* 346 (2014).

6   George Estreich, "Screening the Human Future: YouTube, Persuasion, and Genetically Engineered Children," *Salon*, December 9, 2018, www.salon.com.

7   Rachel Adams, "Gene Edited Babies Don't Grow in Test Tubes," *The Conversation*, May 29, 2019, https://theconversation.com.

8   A. J. Jacobs, *It's All Relative: Adventures Up and Down the World's Family Tree* (New York: Simon and Schuster, 2017).

9 Heather Murphy, "How White Nationalists See What They Want to See in DNA Tests," *New York Times*, July 12, 2019, www.nytimes.com; Aaron Panofsky, "Genetic Ancestry Testing among White Nationalists," *Social Studies of Science* July 2, 2019, https://journals.sagepub.com.

10 Bijal P. Trivedi, "Is Health Care Ready for Routine DNA Screening?," *Science*, October 26, 2017, www.sciencemag.org; Kathleen McGlone West, Erica Blacksher, and Wylie Burke, "Genomics, Health Disparities, and Missed Opportunities for the Nation's Research Agenda," *JAMA*, May 9, 2017, www.ncbi.nlm.nih.gov.

11 Alison Piepmeier, "Outlawing Abortion Won't Help Children with Down Syndrome," *New York Times*, April 1, 2013, https://parenting.blogs.nytimes.com.

12 Anne Wafula Strike, "Disabled Women See #MeToo and Think What about Us?," *Guardian*, March 8, 2018, www.theguardian.com; Holly Kearl, "People with Disabilities Have Been Left Out of Conversations about Harassment," *Huffington Post*, March 17, 2018, www.huffpost.com.

13 Amanda Sakuma, "A Woman in a Vegetative State Suddenly Gave Birth. Her Alleged Assault Is a #MeToo Wakeup Call," *Vox*, January 7, 2019, www.vox.com.

14 Blake Ellis and Melanie Hicken, "Sick, Dying and Raped in America's Nursing Homes," *CNN*, February 22, 2017, www.cnn.com.

15 Erica Harrell, quoted in Joseph Shapiro, "The Sexual Assault Epidemic No One Talks About," Abused and Betrayed Series, *NPR*, January 8, 2018, www.npr.org.

16 Kathy Eddy, *Sexuality and People with Mental Disabilities: The Issues, the Law, and the Guardian* (Bellefonte, PA: National Guardianship Association, 2007); W. Kempton and E. Kahn, "Sexuality and People with Intellectual Disabilities: A Historical Perspective." *Sexuality and Disability* 9.2: 93–110; Ruth Luckasson and Leslie Walker Hirsch, "Consent to Sexual Activity: Legal and Clinical Considerations" in *The Facts of Life . . . and More: Sexuality and Intimacy for People with Intellectual Disabilities*, ed. Leslie Walker-Hirsch (Baltimore: Paul H. Brookes Publishing, 2007), 179–192.

17 Joseph Shapiro, "For Some with Intellectual Disabilities, Ending Abuse Starts with Sex Ed," Abused and Betrayed Series, *NPR*, January 9, 2018, www.npr.org.

18 Tom Shakespeare, "Love, Friendship, Intimacy," in *Disability Rights and Wrongs*, 167–184 (New York and London: Routledge, 2006).

19 Rachel Adams, "Privacy, Dependency, Discegenation: Toward a Sexual Culture for People with Intellectual Disabilities," *Disability Studies Quarterly* 35, no. 1 (2015), http://dsq-sds.org.

20 Michel Desjardins, "The Sexualized Body of the Child: Parents and the Politics of 'Voluntary' Sterilization of People Labeled Intellectually Disabled," in *Sex and Disability*, ed. Robert McRuer and Anna Mollow, 69–88 (Durham, NC: Duke University Press, 2012).

21 Sarah F. Rose, *No Right to Be Idle: The Invention of Disability, 1840s–1930s* (Chapel Hill: University of North Carolina Press, 2017).

22 Julia A. Rivera Drew, "Disability, Poverty, and Material Hardship Since the Passage of the ADA," *Disability Studies Quarterly* 35, no.3 (2015), http://dsq-sds.org; World Health Organization, *World Report on Disability* (Geneva: WHO Library, 2011).

23 Jane Bernstein, "Why Are People Trying to Take My Disabled Daughter's Job Away?," *Vice*, May 1, 2016, www.vice.com.

24 Susan Sontag, *Illness as Metaphor* (New York: Farrar, Straus, Giroux, 1978).

25 Alison Piepmeier, "Thank You for My Beautiful Life," *Charleston City Paper*, July 20, 2016, www.charlestoncitypaper.com.

26 Atul Gawande, *Being Mortal: Medicine and What Matters in the End* (New York: Picador, 2014).

27 Alison Piepmeier, Amber Cantrell, and Ashley Maggio, "Disability Is a Feminist Issue: Bringing Together Women's and Gender Studies and Disability Studies," *Disability Studies Quarterly* 34, no. 2 (2014), http://dsq-sds.org.

BIBLIOGRAPHY

Bernstein, Jane. *Loving Rachel: A Family's Journey from Grief.* Urbana: University of Illinois Press, 1988.

———. *Rachel in the World.* Urbana: University of Illinois Press, 2007.

Bérubé, Michael. "Equality, Freedom, and/or Justice for All: A Response to Martha Nussbaum." *Cognitive Disability and Its Challenge to Moral Philosophy*, edited by Eva Feder Kittay and Licia Carlson, 97–109. West Sussex, UK: Wiley-Blackwell, 2010.

———. *Life as We Know It: A Father, a Family, and an Exceptional Child.* New York: Vintage Books, 1996.

Collins, Paul. *Not Even Wrong: A Father's Journey into the Lost History of Autism.* New York: Bloomsbury, 2004.

Couser, G. Thomas. *Signifying Bodies: Disability in Contemporary Life Writing.* Ann Arbor: University of Michigan Press, 2009.

———. *Vulnerable Subjects: Ethics and Life Writing.* Ithaca, NY: Cornell University Press, 2004.

Forman, Vicki. *This Lovely Life: A Memoir of Premature Motherhood.* Boston: Mariner Books, 2009.

Fournier, Jean-Louis. *Where We Going, Daddy? Life with Two Sons Unlike Any Others.* New York: Other Press, 2008.

Ginsburg, Faye, and Rayna Rapp. "Enabling Disability: Rewriting Kinship, Reimagining Citizenship." In *Going Public: Feminism and the Shifting Boundaries of the Private Sphere*, edited by Joan W. Scott and Debra Keates, 178–200. Urbana: University of Illinois Press, 2004.

Groneberg, Jennifer Graf. *Road Map to Holland: How I Found My Way Through My Son's First Two Years with Down Syndrome.* New York: New American Library, 2008.

Johnson, Harriet McBryde. *Too Late to Die Young: Nearly True Tales from a Life.* New York: Picador, 2005.

Kephart, Beth. *A Slant of Sun: One Child's Courage.* New York: Quill, 1998.

Kittay, Eva Feder. *Love's Labor: Essays on Women, Equality, and Dependency.* New York: Routledge, 1999.

———. "When Caring Is Just and Justice Is Caring: Justice and Mental Retardation." *Public Culture* 13, no. 3 (2001): 557–579.

Landsman, Gail Heidi. *Reconstructing Motherhood and Disability in the Age of "Perfect" Babies*. New York: Routledge, 2008.

McLaughlin, Janice, Dan Goodley, Emma Clavering, and Pamela Fisher. *Families Raising Disabled Children: Enabling Care and Social Justice*. London: Palgrave Macmillan, 2008.

Mills, Bruce. "Nothing about Us, without Us." Review of *Weather Reports from the Autism Front: A Father's Memoir of His Autistic Son* by James C. Wilson and *The Only Boy in the World: A Father Explores the Mysteries of Autism* by Michael Blastland." *Disability Studies Quarterly* 30, no. 1 (2010), www.dsq-sds.org.

Mintz, Susannah B. "Side by Side: Life-Writers on Disabled Siblings." In *New Essays on Life Writing and the Body*, edited by Christopher Stuart and Stephanie Todd, 241–260. Newcastle upon Tyne: Cambridge Scholars Publishing, 2009.

———. *Unruly Bodies: Life Writing by Women with Disabilities*. Chapel Hill: University of North Carolina Press, 2007.

Mont, Daniel. *A Different Kind of Boy: A Father's Memoir about Raising a Gifted Child with Autism*. Philadelphia: Jessica Kingsley Publishers, 2002.

Moore, Charlotte. *George & Sam: Two Boys, One Family, and Autism*. New York: St. Martin's Griffin, 2004.

Park, Clara Claiborne. *Exiting Nirvana: A Daughter's Life with Autism*. Boston: Little, Brown and Company, 2001.

———. *The Siege: A Family's Journey into the World of an Autistic Child*. Boston: Little, Brown and Company, 1967.

Piepmeier, Alison. "What a Shattered Coffee Cup Says about Life." *Charleston City Paper*. June 2, 2016. www.charlestoncitypaper.com.

Rummel-Hudson, Robert. *Schuyler's Monster: A Father's Journey with His Wordless Daughter*. New York: St. Martin's Griffin, 2008.

Savarese, Emily Thornton, and Ralph James Savarese. "'The Superior Half of Speaking': An Introduction." *Disability Studies Quarterly* 30, no. 1 (2010), www.dsq-sds.org.

Savarese, Ralph James. *Reasonable People: A Memoir of Autism and Adoption*. New York: Other Press, 2007.

Soper, Kathryn Lynard. *The Year My Son and I Were Born: A Story of Down Syndrome, Motherhood, and Self-Discovery*. Guilford, CT: Globe Pequot Press, 2009.

INDEX

Aasha (parent), 60–63
able-bodied people, xi, 7
ableism, 58, 90
abortion, 1, 4, 20–21, 24, 129, 134; access
    to, 47, 59; bans on, 39; as choice,
    52–56; disability and, 31–38, 43; Kafer
    on, 146n27; prenatal testing and, 37;
    right to, 38–39, 56, 107, 146n30; selec-
    tive, 38, 40. *See also* termination, of
    pregnancy
abortion laws, 58, 64, 129
acceptance, 6, 65; of autism, 95; from
    parents, 99
access, 104; to abortion, 47, 59; to prenatal
    testing, 33
accommodation, 78
accomplishments, 98
activism, 10–11, 13; advocacy to, 17, 18;
    memoirs as, 100; by parents, 22. *See
    also* reproductive justice
Adams, Rachel, ix, xii, xxiii
adoption, 39, 94, 98, 107
adults: disabled, 77; with Down syndrome,
    74–75
advocacy: to activism, 17, 18; parental,
    83–84
AFP (alpha-fetoprotein), 41; test for, 144n9
alcohol, 48
"Alison's New Hair" (Piepmeier), 111–12
alpha-fetoprotein. *See* AFP
Alzheimer's disease, 107
Ammons, A. R., 118

amniocentesis, 2–3, 4, 31, 43, 126, 136
ancestry, genetic testing for, 125–26, 127;
    white supremacy and, 128
Anderson, Laurie, 118
Annual Education Meeting of the Na-
    tional Society for Genetic Counselors,
    107, 111
art, 133
Asch, Adrienne, 62, 144n8
assault, sexual, 129–30
at the table, 72, 78. *See also* welcome table
attitudes, cultural, 90
authors, posthumous, xvii
autism spectrum, 85–86, 91–93, 98, 132–33,
    148n7; acceptance of, 95; Collins on, 95;
    Moore on, 99; Savarese on, 94–95
awards, for memoirs, 147n5 (chap. 4)

bans, on abortion, 39
Beggars and Choosers (Solinger), 146n30
Being Mortal (Gawande), 135
beliefs, religious, 51–52; Christian, 16
Bender, Karen, 39–40
Bernstein, Jane, 86, 92, 97–98, 132, 147n5
    (chap. 4)
Bertelli, Yantra, 148n7
Bérubé, Jamie, 97–98, 133
Bérubé, Michael, 27, 77–78, 83, 97, 147n5
    (chap. 4), 148n12
betrayal, 16
"Beyond Pro-Choice Versus Pro-Life"
    (Smith), 146n30

ABOUT ALISON PIEPMEIER

BRIAN MCGEE

Alison Piepmeier was a writer, a professor, a mother, an activist, a wife, a mentor, a daughter, a feminist, and a friend. At the time of her death from brain cancer in 2016, she was Professor of Women's and Gender Studies at the College of Charleston in South Carolina. She was and is greatly loved.

Alison was born and grew up in Cookeville, Tennessee. She attended Tennessee Technological University and went on to earn a doctoral degree in English from Vanderbilt University, where she also taught for several years as a member of the Vanderbilt faculty. Alison then joined the College of Charleston as Director of the Women's and Gender Studies Program, a position she would hold for the next decade. In that role, she successfully led the effort to create a separate academic major in women's and gender studies at the College of Charleston.

Alison was the author or editor of three books, the first, *Out in Public: Configurations of Women's Bodies in Nineteenth-Century America*; the second, an edited volume, *Catching a Wave: Reclaiming Feminism for the 21st Century*; and the third, *Girl Zines: Making Media, Doing Feminism*. She published many academic articles and was a guest lecturer or scholar at several universities. Alison was a former officer of the National Women's Studies Association and a former president of the Southeastern Women's Studies Association.

In 2008, she gave birth to her daughter, Maybelle, who she adored and, as she once wrote, "loved more than she can imagine it's possible to love anyone." Maybelle is the inspiration for much of this book.

Alison was best known in Charleston for her column on Southern feminism in the *Charleston City Paper*. Her final column, in which she acknowledged her imminent death and expressed thanks for her "beautiful life," was widely read online and led to stories at abcnews.com and the website of *Us Weekly*. Her blog, *Every Little Thing*, is posted at alisonpiepmeier.blogspot.com and chronicles a part of her intellectual and personal journey.

In Charleston and nationally, Alison was a frequent media commentator on social justice and on disability. Her columns and academic research were featured in leading print and online news outlets, including the *New York Times*. The online magazine *Charlie* recognized Alison in 2014 as one of the fifty most progressive people in Charleston.

A scholarship has been endowed at the College of Charleston in her honor. The National Women's Studies Association has named a book award for Alison, and the Southeastern Women's Studies Association now has a graduate student award in her memory.

ABOUT GEORGE ESTREICH AND RACHEL ADAMS

George Estreich is the author of *Fables and Futures: Biotechnology, Disability, and the Stories We Tell Ourselves*. His memoir about raising a daughter with Down syndrome, *The Shape of the Eye*, won the 2012 Oregon Book Award in Creative Nonfiction. He lives in Oregon with his family.

Rachel Adams is Professor of English and Comparative Literature at Columbia University. She is the author of *Raising Henry: A Memoir of Motherhood, Disability, and Discovery*; *Continental Divides: Remapping the Cultures of North America*; and *Sideshow U.S.A.: Freaks and the American Cultural Imagination*. She is co-editor of *Keywords for Disability Studies*. She is a Guggenheim fellow for 2019–2020.